AVRO LANCASTER

MIDLAND

An imprint of
Ian Allan Publishing

AVRO LANCASTER
Britain's Greatest Wartime Bomber

PETER C SMITH

Author's Note

The philosophy of Lord Trenchard had long dominated the thinking of the Royal Air Force in the two-decade period from 1919 to 1939, now known retrospectively as 'Between the Wars'. As a newly independent service the RAF was eager to establish a totally new and original doctrine to justify its hard-won status. Gradually, as the reliability and size of military aircraft developed, the acceptance of a long-range air striking force able to devastate any enemy war plant and infrastructure and thus bring any war to a successful termination without the huge loss of life engendered by land and sea battles of the conventional type, emerged. It is often forgotten that, initially anyway, France was considered as Great Britain's main potential enemy in the air, for Germany was prostrate and seemed destined to remain so. Range therefore was not so much of a problem as it later became for this type of planned aerial bombardment when, resurgent under a new and militaristic leader, Germany once again re-emerged as the principal probable opponent in the 1930s.

A decade and a half of the neglect of national defence forced upon all three services by a succession of introspective Governments and, especially, a myopic Treasury, could not be rectified in a few years; and with all three services competing for very limited funds, money had to be spread thinly. Despite this, some new aircraft were provided for the RAF's bomber arm, such as the Handley-Page Hampden, the Vickers Wellington and the Short Stirling; but with the swift overrunning of Western Europe by the Germans, these aircraft either lacked the range or the increasingly necessary payload to make the strategic air campaign, now the only way to hit back at the German war machine, a viable concept. A new solution had to be found, and, forced through by the total single-mindedness of Air Marshal Arthur Travis Harris and (initially) the enthusiastic backing of Premier Winston Churchill, the design team at Avro came up with the ultimate World War II bombing machine, the Avro Lancaster. This is her story.

Peter C. Smith
May 2008

First published 2008

ISBN 978 85780 269 6

Project Editor and Production: Chevron Publishing Limited
© Colour profiles and graphics: Tim Brown
Chevron Publishing would like to thank Mark Postlethwaite for his co-operation in the production of this book.

Published by Midland Publishing
An imprint of Ian Allan Publishing Ltd, Riverside Business Park, Molesey Road, Hersham, Surrey, KT12 4RG
Printed by Ian Allan Printing Ltd, Riverside Business Park, Molesey Road, Hersham, Surrey, KT12 4RG

Code: 0807/D1

Visit the Ian Allan Publishing website at **www.ianallanpublishing.co.uk**

CONTENTS

FOREWORD

Ron Clark, DFC, Lancaster pilot, 'The Phantom of the Ruhr', No.100 Squadron

Pilot Officer Ron Clark, DFC, No.100 Squadron, RAF Waltham, Linconshire, 1943.

BEING new boys after our arrival at No.100 Squadron at RAF Waltham near Grimsby in late May 1943, we were surprised to be assigned a brand new Lancaster Mk.III. She was a good example of the type, and someone had pencilled on the back of the armour plate behind the pilots seat 'May good luck follow you always'.

The Lancaster was pleasant to fly, being light on the controls, but could be a bit skittish landing on the main wheels instead of a three-pointer after any slight misjudgement.

We had a week of local flying before our first operation to Düsseldorf. Entering the briefing room, I saw that I was bottom of the list of captains on the Battle Order. When one of them was erased, the rest of us moved up a notch. Of course sometimes the bottom one was rubbed out, but it was idle to speculate about one's progress up the list.

Loaded as we were with H.E., incendiaries, ammunition and 1,600 gallons of fuel, it was our first heavy weight take-off and we needed most of the runway. We left the assembly point at Mablethorpe on the coast at 22,000 feet and darkness soon fell as we headed away from the sun. An unexpected experience was the occasional lurch as we flew into the slipstream of unseen Lancasters ahead with no navigation lights on.

Night fighters usually came in from behind and below and we relied on Geoff Green in the rear turret to spot them. It was much easier for them to see us with our flaming exhausts, than it was for us to pick out the small shapes in the starlight. In moonlight it was easier for everybody! From a distance the flak barrage over the target was like a bunch of firework sparklers, along with the probing searchlights and gun flashes. Doug Wheeler, our bomb aimer, had the best view of the inferno below and was it was up to me to keep the aircraft steady on the bombing run. After he called 'Bombs Gone', the Lanc became much livelier and we turned away for home.

Following a few trips, we decided on the name 'Phantom of the Ruhr' for EE139, the film 'Phantom of the Opera' which was showing at the time. Ben Bennett, our flight engineer, was given a free hand with the paintbrush to produce something appropriate on the nose.

The Lancaster could absorb a good deal of punishment, which was well demonstrated over Mannheim on the night of 27 September 1943. We were coned by searchlights and subjected to heavy flak and a direct hit from a shell which exploded above us, on the way passing through the tail of the 'cookie', narrowly missing Lish Easby, our wireless operator, and jamming our aileron control wires. This put us in an out-of-control vertical spiral. Ben and I managed to wrench the controls free, but we were left with partial control and wing flutter. All this put considerable stress on the airframe and on recovery to straight and level flight, a fighter attacked, which caused further

Right: Ron Clark (centre) with some of his crew and ground staff members, No.100 Squadron, RAF Waltham 1943.

Far right: The original 'Phantom of the Ruhr', Lancaster Mk.III, EE139, as painted by Ben Bennett, Ron Clark's flight engineer, photographed at RAF Waltham in 1943.

Below right: Ron Clark with the Battle of Britain Memorial Flight's Lancaster, PA474, in the colours of his 'Phantom of the Ruhr' at No.100 Squadron, RAF Leeming, June 2007.

damage to the right wing and flaps. After evasive action with the aircraft shaking and at low altitude we were now in danger from bombs being dropped from above. Ben had worked out the cause of the wing flutter and delved into the control pedestal where with the help of the glare from the searchlights found the aileron trimming wires still attached and severed them. The shaking stopped at once and the Lanc got us safely home.

That was our last operation with her as she was out of action for a couple of months and we took our farewells in the hangar the next morning. The ground crew found the tail of an incendiary bomb lodged in one of the engine intakes, the explosive part being neatly removed by one of the propeller blades, which had a dent in it.

The 'Phantom of the Ruhr' however went on to be one of the thirty-five Lancasters to complete a hundred or more operations, the final tally being 120[1]. She was the only aircraft I ever had a personal relationship with and she was 'resurrected' by the Battle of Britain Memorial Flight two years ago. Their Lancaster is painted in the livery of my old aircraft, 'Phantom of the Ruhr' which is in great demand up and down the country during the air show season.

[1] 'Phantom of the Ruhr', after her spell with No.100 Squadron, passed to No.550 Squadron (formed from 'C' Flight of No.100 Squadron in November 1943). Then to 1656 and 1660 HCUs (Heavy Conversion Units), until finally being SOC (Struck of charge) on 12 January 1946, after flying a total of 830+hours.

1 The Task and the Requirement

Although for twenty years the Royal Air Force had concentrated its main thrust and purpose on the establishment of a strategic bombing force – to the almost total exclusion of all else, including modern fighters, close air support and maritime operations, all of which were regarded as irrelevant – early missions in the Second World War quickly revealed that existent heavy bombers had neither the accuracy, the lifting power nor the range either to conduct daylight operations without unacceptable losses, or nocturnal operations with any degree of accuracy. Not only new technology had to be found, but also a much improved weapons platform.

Left: A Whitley of No. 78 Squadron is prepared for a night operation over Germany in early 1941.

Below: Of the three bomber types that bore the brunt of the RAF bomber offensive during the first three years of war, the Whitley had the lowest performance. This example, a Mark V, belonged to No. 102 Squadron based at Finningley in Yorkshire before the war. At the outbreak of war the type was relegated to the role of night raider, and it flew many of the early leaflet-dropping missions over Germany.

THE gap between the universally held view of the Air Marshals that strategic bombing was the only worthwhile *raison d'être*, and what was accomplished between 1940 and 1942, was a vast one. Bravery and persistence did not come into it since there was plenty of both from the aircrews; but achievements were large illusionary, no matter what spin the dictates of propaganda on British morale put on the facts. It mattered more that the heavy bomber was the only way to hit back at the Germans in this period than the fact that target-finding, let alone target-annihilation, was clearly not being achieved.

Not only was the supremacy of the heavy bomber an uncritical article of faith among the leaders of the Royal Air Force, but it was also a widely-held view among its civilian supporters pre-war. The Italian General Douhet had, in his much-quoted treatise, *The Command of the Air*, preached that the only effective way to destroy an enemy's firepower was to bomb his airfields, supply bases and factories thus eliminating all at source. The 'father' of the Royal Air Force, Lord Trenchard, was even more outspoken and his doctrine of taking the air war to the enemy by creating a heavy bomber force that would carry all before it from the very outset of war, saw total victory achievable by this method alone. Even politicians fell into line and Prime Minister Balfour's famous statement that, "the bomber would always get through" justified lack of expenditure on defensive measures.

Even such a widely-read writer as former Air Commodore Lionel Evely Oswald Charlton, who had resigned his job in Iraq after witnessing the effect of bombing civilians, was to aver in his 1937 book *The Menace of the Clouds*, that, "Air power is bombing capacity and nothing else", adding, "An assessment of the air strength of a country should be based exclusively on the weight-carrying capacity, the speed, the range, and on the number of its bomber squadrons." Interestingly a certain A T Harris[1], who displayed no such squeamish reservations, had replaced Charlton.

The Air Ministry totally agreed with such sentiments, despite the fact that pre-war bombing exercises like those held that same year showed a lamentable lack of accuracy and destructive achievement, even after a week of bombing stationary targets; while a pre-war study into the feasibility of constructing the required fleet of four-engined bombers to put Lord Trenchard's vision into practice had concluded that it was totally prohibitive.

Forced into acceptance of the Trenchard doctrine by Britain's swift and humiliating ejection from Continental Europe, the RAF lacked the means, but by no means the will, to carry it out. Churchill embraced the concept wholeheartedly, stating that, "Bombers alone

[1] Harris later received the epithet "Bomber" from the Press, although his aircrews' nickname for him was "Butch" for Butcher (of the enemy and of themselves) even though they enormously admired him as their leader for his staunchness and single-mindedness of purpose.

morale of the German people to a point where their armed resistance is fatally weakened."

The arrival of Arthur Harris as the new Commander-in-Chief of Bomber Command in 1942, ensured a single-minded commitment to the achievement of the new policy. Expansion of Bomber Command was no longer considered 'unfeasible'; instead everything was seconded to it and up to 50 per cent of Britain's total war effort was eventually allocated. Churchill himself recorded that even with the disasters of the fall of Singapore and Burma, nothing was to deflect from the new policy. " We have built up a great plant here for bombing Germany..."

This new target allocation also resulted in a change of

provide the means of victory." From October 1940 this air offensive began to gather pace.

German fighter defences quickly saw the abandonment of strategical bombing by daylight by the RAF, but the switch to night attacks also had a penalty. The Butt Report of August 1941 revealed the unpalatable fact that analysis of photographs of Bomber Command targets proved that at least 50 per cent of bombs intended for important industrial targets were, in fact, falling up to five miles away in open countryside.

Another major change of policy resulted with the decision at the highest level to switch target selection from precision targets to area targets in an effort to break German civilian morale. The reasoning behind this was encapsulated by the Combined Chiefs of Staff on 21 January 1943 as, "..the progressive destruction of the German military, industrial and economic system, and the undermining of the

ordnance in order to maximise this effort. For such a new policy to work the enemy had to be struck in his heartland. This clearly required a much more accurate target guidance system and elite Pathfinder units and, later, airborne radar navigation systems were to fill this need. A larger bomb-carrying capacity and new types of ordnance, especially incendiary devices, together with a far greater range than the heavy bomber types then in use or in the pipeline following the adoption of the B.12/36 and P.13/36 pre-war specifications, emerged as the four-engined Handley-Page Halifax and Short Stirling and the twin-engined Avro Manchester. The Vulture-II-engined Manchester was a machine that held out the most promise of development, and the key proved to be the reversion of its power plant back to the original Merlin. It was a turning point.

A new and awesome heavy bomber was about to appear on the scene.

Left: The Handley Page Halifax was the second, of the four engined 'heavies' to enter service, going into action for the first time in March 1941. This Halifax B.II Series I, W7676, TL-P, belonged to No. 35 (Madras Presidency) Squadron and was lost in a night raid against Nuremberg on 28/29 August 1942.

Right: A Halifax of No 192 Squadron, which gathered electronic intelligence on the latest German radio and radar systems.

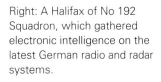

Above: A Stirling of No. 199 Squadron, one of the heavy jamming units of No. 100 Group.

Right: Ground crew prepare to load a Short Stirling of No. 149 Squadron with its 500 lb bombs during the summer of 1942.

2 Inspiration and
Creation

Although the inspired skills of the A. V. Roe team developed the Avro Manchester, which promised much, it turned out to be a blind alley, due, in large part, to the complexity of the Vulture engine around which it had been necessarily designed. However, this apparent setback was transformed in an incredibly short period of time by the same design group and resulted in the best all-round heavy bomber built by any nation during the Second World War.

Left: A Mk.Ia Manchester, which was superseded by the Lancaster, is here being prepared for a mission on 17 April 1942 and is being loaded with two 2,000 lb bombs. The type proved troublesome which was mainly due to the problems encountered by its two Rolls-Royce Vulture engines and was withdrawn from service.

THE Air Ministry Specification P.13/36 had required a twin-engined heavy bomber capable of carrying a total bomb load of 8,000 lb (3,628.73 kg) or a pair of 21-inch (53.34 cm) air-launched torpedoes, with a total crew complement of six including two pilots, with dual controls, a navigator & bomb-aimer, a wireless operator & front gunner, a tail gunner and a ventral gunner. The power plant was to be the Rolls Royce 24-cylinder, liquid-cooled, Vulture of potentially 1,800 hp. The design, which had best met this demanding profile, proved to be the Avro Type 679, which had a wing span of 80 ft (24.38 m).

The long-established Manchester-based firm of Avro had been founded in 1910 by Alliott Verdon Roe and his brother Humphrey Verdon. The company's Chief Designer was Roy Chadwick with

The designer of the Avro Lancaster, Roy Chadwick (right), chats with Wing Commander Guy Gibson outside Buckingham Palace on 22 June 1943.

General Manager Roy Hardy Dobson, both of whom had a long track record of innovative and successful bomber designs dating back to the First World War and in particular the Avro 504. The two new bomber prototypes, soon to be designated the Manchester, were ordered in September 1936, and featured a twin-tail configuration, also adopted by the contemporary Handley-Page Halifax, and undercarriage retracting into the wing-mounted engine nacelles.

The first Manchester was L7246, with her main sections constructed at Newton Heath and finally assembled, without defensive armament, at Ringway airfield. Making her maiden flight in July 1939 with Captain H. A. 'Sam' Brown at the controls, subsequent RAF testing at Boscombe Down was partly successful but revealed a lack of power in the Vulture-I and considerable lateral instability. The second prototype, L7247, sought to rectify these shortcomings by adopting new rudders and an extended outer wing, while the Vulture-I was power-enhanced with unlimited boosting.

When first flown in May 1940, the second machine showed some improvement, but despite the intense pressure to get the machine into production due to the dire war situation then developing, it was not sufficient to warrant a move to full production, even though this had been expected to immediately follow. Therefore L7247 was modified and adapted: a central fin was fitted to try and rectify the lateral difficulties; the improved Vulture-II engine was trialled. The original specification to carry torpedoes had the happy result of requiring a larger than usual bomb bay, a feature which practically guaranteed the further development of the type as mission loads vastly increased.

Defensive armament was also emplaced for more realistic trials, with the three hydraulically operated Nash & Thompson gun turrets designed to cover front, rear and ventral defensive sky arcs. The most powerful turret was the quadruple .303 Browning FN4; the nose defence was provided by the already standard bomber unit, the twin Browning FN5; the under-body FN21 twin-Browning-equipped turret, a relic of the 1930s, and commonly known as the 'dustbin', which aptly described its antiquated appearance, had to be lowered down from the fuselage prior to use with the resultant high airflow drag factor.

Orders totalling some six hundred machines had already been placed, with the first three hundred aircraft to be built by A.V. Roe (as the co-ordinating lead team) and by Metropolitan-Vickers at

Newton Heath and Trafford Park respectively with subcontracted additional airframes placed out to Sir W. G. Armstrong Whitworth and Fairey Aviation Company (known collectively as The Manchester Group). This number of Manchester orders was to double with the pressing necessity of the war.

While urgent improvements were still being made with the second prototype, the first production machine, L7276, was completed and delivered to Boscombe Down in August 1940, followed by a sister, L7277, in October. These machines, which now

A close up of the starboard Rolls-Royce Vulture engine of an Avro Manchester. This engine was principally two Peregrines (supercharged Kestrels) joined at the crankcase, producing an 'X' engine configuration (both engines shared a single crankshaft).

Opposite: Avro Manchester L7515 of 207 Squadron. Despite the type's unreliability, this particular example survived its entire operational career until it was struck off charge in November 1943.

featured a modified central third tail fin, reflected the improvements already achieved and, following intensive testing of the two aircraft, with further minor modifications, full production was continued as a matter of haste and urgency. The first operational squadron to be equipped with the Manchester was No. 207 Squadron RAF, based at Waddington, hitherto a training unit equipped with the sedate and undemanding Avro Anson. Now, as part of No. 5 Group, Bomber Command, this unit was tasked with bringing the new bomber into operational service in the shortest possible time frame, including continuing evaluation and crew familiarisation and training.

In truth the rush into service, although understandable, was premature and the continued overheating and lack of power problems with the Vulture engine, as well as airframe weaknesses, soon began to show. The novel concept behind the Vulture engine was that by combining a pair of 12-cylinder Peregrine engines one above the other in one nacelle, in theory developed horsepower would result, combined with greater weight-saving and space. With only one of these combinations mounted on each wing, there was the bonus of reduced cost in comparison with a more conventional four-engined configuration. Even so, it was recognised as something of a risky concept, so much so that as early as 1938 an alternative proposal by Roy Chadwick to adopt a four-engine status utilising the Merlin engine, as the Avro Type 680, (initially without any increase in wing length), had been touted and considered.

Although the Manchester-I made her operational debut as early as the end of February 1941, she was sent into action still minus any dorsal turret. This was rectified with the arrival of the Nash & Thompson FN7, which held two Browning machine guns. As production mounted, further squadrons were equipped with Manchester-Is but in April the existing force had to be grounded while work on the engine problems was seriously addressed. Opportunity was taken to upgrade the airframe in order to increase bomb capacity from 2,000 lb (907.38 kg) to 4,000 lb (1,814.36 kg) before operations resumed and this weapon was dropped in action by a Manchester bomber for the first time on the night of 2/3 May.

Despite this milestone, losses from engine-related and other causes continued to be high and a second suspension of operations followed in June/July. At one point the aborting of the whole Manchester programme was contemplated, but this would have left a vast gap in Bomber Command's future plans and so further modifications to

The prototype Lancaster, BT308. This aircraft was built up from a Manchester fuselage, and shared the latter's smaller tail fins and single fin. It was fitted with four Merlin X engines in a modified wing with increased rib spacing to give a span of 100 feet. A dorsal turret was not fitted. Performance was as per the Mk.I Lancaster. After first flights and initial tests, the aircraft went to Nos. 44, 97 and 207 Squadrons during late 1941 to early 1942 for familiarisation trials. In April 1942 it passed to Whitworth Aircraft, who fitted a Metrovick F.2/1 jet engine in the tail for flying trials. In the background can be seen a Blackburn Roc, the fighter version of the Blackburn Skua.

The second prototype Lancaster DG595, was painted in the standard daylight scheme of dark earth/dark green with yellow undersides.

Left and right: The second prototype Lancaster DG595, with the larger fins, in flight and at rest. Note the unfaired base to the dorsal turret, fitment of a belly turret and flame dampeners (at right). This aircraft was fitted with Merlin XX engines and following its first flight on 13 May 1941, it went to the A. & A.E.E. for trials. From September to March 1942 it was at the Avro factory for modifications and repair. In early 1943 it went to the R.A.E. for use in ballistic trials. On 20 June 1943, it was damaged by the blast effect thrown up by an inert bomb dropped from 100 feet at Ashley Walk, Hants. It was subsequently repaired and spent its final service life at the Torpedo Development Unit.

improve the reliability of the Vulture were made and eventually it was decided to evaluate replacing this engine with either the in-line Napier Sabre-I or even the radial Bristol Centaurus. The latter was fitted as a trial machine, tentatively designated the Manchester Mk. II, but this development was overtaken by events.

In addition to improving the long-standing lateral problems, the size of the tailplane and two external tail fins was much increased, and the third, central fin was omitted altogether. These changes resulted in the Manchester-IA and offensive combat operations resumed in August 1941. By the end of the year there were four operational squadrons in limited service, taking part in the ongoing and largely abortive attacks on the two German battlecruisers docked at Brest. Manchesters continued to be utilised on operations, including the first three 'Thousand Bomber Raids', but only to make up the numbers and, although fresh units were equipped, their final mission over Germany was conducted on 25/26 June against Bremen.

Production of the Manchester was finally ceased altogether by the Ministry of Aircraft Production after just two hundred Mk I and Mk IA aircraft had rolled off the assembly lines, 157 from Newton Heath and a mere 43 from Trafford Park. Those that remained found useful employment in the secondary, but essential duties of crew training with Heavy Conversion Units (HCUs), where they lingered until 1943. The residue from the original orders, 43 from Newton Heath and 53 from Metropolitan-Vickers, were ultimately to be completed as a new four-engined bomber, while those placed with Fairey and Armstrong Whitworth were terminated totally.

Meanwhile, with the Manchester *impasse* still largely unresolved but with the need more urgent than ever before, the 1938 proposal was taken out and re-examined in earnest. In 1939 Avro's speculative four-engined Manchester was clearly eligible for consideration under the Air Ministry's new B.I/39 Specification, which required a four-engined bomber to carry a 10,000 lb (4,540 kg) bomb load for 2,500 miles (4.023 km), with a seven-man crew, giving an all-up gross weight of 55,000 lbs (30,840 kg). This heavyweight was to be able to cruise at a speed of 261mph (420 km/h) at an altitude of 12,800 ft (3,904 m).

Chadwick was able to reconsider his proposal in the light of this new requirement. The resulting rejig was the Avro Type 683 which saw four Merlin X engines being mounted on a lengthened wing, (an increase from 80 ft [24.3 m] to 102 ft [31.09 m] in overall wingspan), and a greatly enlarged 33 ft (10.6 m) tailplane. Due to pressure to get the Manchester into service, this intriguing rework was hived off to a separate development team under Stuart Davies.

Work necessarily proceeded at a slow pace but, even before the cancellation of the Manchester contracts, with the writing-off of the Vulture engine in 1940, the Avro team was animated by the rumour of being turned into a subcontractor for the Halifax. They sought and gained an audience with MAP in which their Type 683, with the Manchester's roomy bomb stowage and proven existent airframe, as positive and proven features, was forwarded as worthy of a second consideration. They were rewarded for their perseverance and faith, with contracts awarded in November to proceed with one specific prototype, (as the Manchester III), with three further different but unspecified prototypes, to see how their new concept fitted with the Air Ministry's requirement.

To provide the first prototype, which Chadwick and Davies had already decided would incorporate as much of the 'standard' Manchester design as possible, a production line Mk. I airframe, BT308, was earmarked for conversion. This aircraft was specifically required to be powered by four Rolls Royce Merlin X engines and, to accommodate the two extra outboard nacelles, new outer wing assemblies were required. The two inner engines were fitted in exactly the same positions as on the Manchester, although their nacelles had to be slightly modified to allow for the different shape of the Merlin. This also required some adjustments to the assembly line jigs, but these proved relatively easy to alter.

The Manchester electrical system was retained, utilising a pair of generators driven by the inner engines as before. Likewise, the hydraulics and pneumatics were initially to remain unaltered, but, of course, the fuel system had to be modified considerably to accommodate the two additional engines. Two extra throttle controls necessitated some reworking of the cockpit layout and to accommodate a doubling of the instrument console width, the controls for the propellers were displaced to an underneath location.

To balance the additional weight the enlarged 33 ft (10.6 m) tailplane, as already trialled on the Manchester, was fitted and the central fin made a brief reappearance, but all other fittings remained as standard. Surprisingly, no changes were considered necessary to the undercarriage. However, during the conversion some adjustments were found necessary to the hydraulics, which caused a brief delay before flight-testing. Only the nose and rear gun turrets were installed in this machine, however. The maiden flight of the first prototype, flown by Capt. Brown and Bill Thorn, therefore did not take place until 9 January 1941.

Following a succession of test flights from the Ringway field BT308 was transferred to Boscombe Down at the end of the month for A&AEE flight trialling. The rigorous flight programme revealed that the new aircraft was a sound proposition overall, but there was still the old problem with directional stability and the aircraft was returned to the plant for the fitting of the new tail section, while the central fin was dropped from the design. Further testing continued with this machine during the summer.

A post-war photograph of engine mechanics working on a Merlin engine on a Lancaster at Tuddenham in July 1946. Despite this this view being taken post-war it typifies the scene on wartime Bomber Command bases where the groundcrews worked in all weathers to keep the aircraft flying - a task that should not be forgotten by all.

Left: An unusual view of a
Lancaster Mk.II seen from the
front showing its Bristol Hercules
radial engines.

Above: 426 (Thunderbird)
Squadron, RCAF, operating from
Linton-on-Ouse, was one of the
few squadrons that flew the
Armstrong-Whitworth-built and
Bristol Hercules-powered
Lancaster B Mk.II between July
1943 and May 1944. Seen here
in the summer of 1943, OW-S,
DS689, commanded by F/Sgt.
M.B. Summers, was lost in
action when it crashed in France
following a raid to Stuttgart on
7 October that year. The damage
to the city however, as a result of
that raid, was considerable, with
344 buildings destroyed and
another 4,586 damaged.

Left: Lancaster Mk.II DS771 seen
on a test flight before delivery to
426 (Thunderbird) Squadron,
RCAF. The aircraft would be lost
over Stuttgart on 15 March 1944.

Cut-away view of a Merlin XX. It produced 1,480 hp (1,105 kW) at 3,000 rpm at 6,000 ft (1,830 m). It was used in the Hurricane Mk.II, Beaufighter Mk.II fighters, Halifax Mk.II and Lancaster Mk.I bombers.

electrical requirements and this was carried out at Woodford (near Stockport) prior to transfer to Boscombe Down flight evaluation in August 1941.

The Merlin engine was a great success and became the standard power plant. The main difficulty reported with this very reliable power plant was the heavy vibration the four engines set up across the Lancaster's airframe. Keeping the engines synchronised mitigated this, but it was not an easy thing to do. Eventually Avro developed a simple instrument to help achieve this, known as the 'Synchroscope' but, although successful, it was not even tested until 1945 and the war ended before it was widely introduced. Meanwhile the Merlin's reliability meant that this engine was also in great demand for powering single-engined fighter aircraft as well as other heavy bombers. Fears were expressed in top circles that demand might well exceed supply, especially with the enormous expansion of Bomber Command. It was deemed prudent and sensible to have an alternative engine established and proven to keep the assembly lines at full stretch and the two-row, fourteen-cylinder, sleeve-valve, air-cooled radial Bristol Hercules VI, developing 1,615 hp and equipped with the two-speed centrifugal supercharger was selected. The third prototype airframe, DT810, was thus equipped with this engine as the lead aircraft for what was the Lancaster Mk. II.

The third prototype was thus not ready for her maiden flight until well after the first Lancaster-I had taken to the air, but flew successfully at the end of November 1941, before also moving on to Boscombe in early 1942 for A&AEE trials. The Hercules engine, being a radial, was, not unexpectedly, found to cause greater drag than the in-line Merlin, but it was of greater power which somewhat compensated, although both increased fuel consumption which had some knock-on effect on range. The Hercules also proved more sensitive to control and required careful nursing. However, it proved adequate enough for the Mk. II production line to be initiated and the first two Mk. IIs were completed in the late summer of 1942. Many were constructed with the ventral gun turret but it proved almost useless against German night fighters in actual combat conditions. Much later Lancasters were equipped with a radar-aimed turret (Automatic Gun Laying Turret or AGLT, known also as 'Village Inn'). This could detect an incoming enemy fighter at a range of 1,400 yds (1,280 m) and hold contact down to 150 yds (137 m). The first Lancaster equipped with this weapon joined No. 460 Squadron

Meanwhile, in the middle of May 1941, the first prototype had been joined by the second, made over at Newton Heath from airframe DG595. By this time the design had received a new name, used at first unofficially at Avro but by the end of February 'adopted' officially by the Royal Air Force, the Lancaster. It was a name destined to become famed in military aeronautical history. This aircraft featured a changed power plant and four twelve-cylinder, 60-degree upright vee, liquid-cooled in-line Merlin XX engines, each having an integral single-stage centrifugal supercharger.

DG595 was especially constructed to be as near to the planned production aircraft as could be attained and thus was fully equipped with all four defensive gun turrets with the addition of the usual Nash & Thompson FN50 in the dorsal position and the inclusion of the FN64 turret in the ventral emplacement. Offensive war-loading was attained and the aircraft was stressed to its 60,000 lb (27,215.54 kg) top weight for her maiden flight, which took place on 13 May. An upgrading of the engine-driven generators to 1,500 watts was deemed necessary in anticipation of the installation of additional

Opposite: The Lancaster B.Is of No. 207 Squadron took part in many of the early Lancaster operations, the unit having received the type in March 1942. The Lancaster nearest the camera, R5570, EM-F, was lost on a raid on Turin on the 8/9 December 1942.

Right: A perfectly framed photograph of No. 419 Squadron Lancaster, KB745, VR-V, taken by the automatic bombing camera from another aircraft over Normandy, in the summer of 1944. Neither pilot was aware of the other until the photographs were developed.

in June 1944 and later one squadron from No. 1 Group and one from No. 5 Group were so allocated.

Another identifying feature on many of the Lancaster-IIs was the fitting of distinctive bulged bomb bay doors, but their appearance was otherwise generally similar. The introduction of the Hercules XVI engine improved performance further but as the feared shortage of the Merlin did not, in fact, materialise, it was not necessary to continue with the Mk. II beyond the single initial order of three hundred aircraft.

Two contracts were placed for Lancaster-IIs with Sir W. G. Armstrong and were constructed at their Whitley plant. The first pair of this variant, DS601 and DS602, arrived at the A&AEE for evaluation. Subsequently squadron deliveries began, with No.61 Squadron at Syderston the first to receive them in the winter of 1942, with the first mission being undertaken in January 1943.

Meanwhile the fourth prototype of the initial contract, the exact specification of which was never drawn up in any detail, and to which airframe DT812 had been allocated, was abandoned and never proceeded with, since the Merlin-equipped Lancaster had turned out to be so satisfactory.

With the anticipation of high numbers of the new bomber being required, the Manchester Group of producers, which by this time had been joined by Vickers Armstrong at Castle Bromwich in the West Midlands, became, in September 1941, the Lancaster Group. Later expansion saw further companies incorporated – Vickers' plant at Chester and Austin Aero, a subsidiary of the Austin Motor Company, based at Longbridge, Birmingham.

It was not until the last day of October 1941, however, that the first fruits of the reorganisation materialised, with the maiden flight of L7527, a Newton Heath Manchester airframe converted to the very first production Lancaster-I. Flight-testing proved generally satisfactory, surviving even a crash-landing, but the uselessness of the FN64 ventral machine gun mounting was agreed upon and this feature was removed from the production line. This reduced the Lancaster's defensive armament to a total of eight .303s, identical to the older Stirling bomber and the early Halifax, whose later models carried an extra gun. Although in 1942 such limited protection, both in terms of numbers and of effective calibre, might have seemed sufficient, it was to prove woefully inadequate once the German night fighter defences started to improve. By Christmas Eve evaluation tests

at the A&AEE had proved the soundness of the overall design and engines and the Lancaster-I was pronounced suitable for combat.

The first RAF squadron to start equipping with the Lancaster was No.44 (Rhodesian) Squadron at Waddington under the acting command of Flight Commander Squadron Leader John Nettleton, which switched over from the already obsolescent Handley-Page Hampden. This involved considerable reorganisation due not just to a vastly different aircraft, bomb loads and fuel requirements, but the need for a larger aircrew and ground personnel complement. Perhaps because of these difficulties, the second unit to receive the Lancaster was an existing Manchester outfit, No. 97 Squadron based at Coningsby, and they duly took delivery of the first one in mid-

The seven crew members of this Lancaster belonging to No. 44 Squadron appear relieved after returning from a raid to Berlin on 2 March 1943.

This Canadian-built Mk.X KB783 was used by the A&AEE to test the Martin mid-upper turret. Note the bulged bomb doors.

January 1942. A third squadron assigned the Lancaster was also a Manchester-equipped squadron, No. 207 at Bottesford.

A milestone in the Lancaster story took place on 3/4 March 1942, when No.44 Squadron despatched a quartet of its new bombers on their first combat assignment, an aerial minelaying mission off Heligoland from which all four aircraft returned safely.

Until the huge industrial might of the United States became actively involved in the war on its own account, British orders enabled them to tool up in readiness and with their massive involvement, free of any danger of damage, the bottleneck of supply of all types of British war materiel considerably eased. The supply of sufficient Merlin engines for example, was hugely facilitated by the introduction into service of the licence-built variant built by the Packard Motor Corporation. These Merlin 28 engines were marginally superior in output from the Rolls Royce-built types; the carburettor and magnetos were different, but in most other respects were almost identical and caused no fitting problems once they started to arrive by freighter across the U-boat infested North Atlantic toward the end of 1942.

Similar trans-Atlantic co-operation also affected airframe production with the establishment of the Victory Aircraft Limited facility set up in a former steel plant at Malton in Ontario, Canada, which began producing the Lancaster in increasing numbers – aptly enough, for the percentage of Canadian aircrews in Bomber Command was also to show a marked rise as the war continued. The first Canadian-built Lancasters, which were designated the Mark X, crossed the Atlantic in September 1943, and ultimately twelve Royal Canadian Air Force Squadrons were equipped with Lancasters in No. 6 Group.

The first Lancaster to be fitted at Newton Heath with these American-built engines was an existing Avro-built Mark I aircraft, W4114, in September 1942. She duly went to Boscombe Down the following month for the usual trials. The Packard-Merlin proved itself more reliable in the long-term, with regard to fuel supply problems, and Mk.Is were often converted to Mk.IIIs as worn-out or malfunctioning engines were replaced. Overall the Lancaster rapidly established itself as the mainstay of the vastly expanded Bomber Command, and, despite month-on-month heavy casualties averaging

A close up of the 'Upkeep' mine in position under the specially modified fuselage of Guy Gibson's Lancaster, ED932, AJ-G. Here the special mounting for the mine and belt drive which spun the weapon to its release speed of 500 rpm is clearly visible.

Opposite: A dramatic view of a No. 279 Squadron Lancaster ASRIII releasing an airborne lifeboat.

twenty-five plus numerous accidental and damage losses, the Lancaster-equipped squadrons mushroomed. On the first anniversary of the Lancaster's introduction into service no fewer than eighteen squadrons were flying this aircraft, and by July a further five squadrons were formed, each with a strength of twenty-five operation aircraft.

By the end of 1943 a further six squadrons had swelled the ranks and, despite write-offs from all factors, production at the various plants managed to keep pace. By the autumn of 1944 three hundred Lancasters a month were pouring from production lines in both the UK and Canada.

Apart from this growing stream of 'standard' models, Mk.1s and Mk.IIIs, was the specialist nature of some of the new ordnance coming into service, much of it designed with specific missions in mind, like the famous 'Dams' attacks, Operation *Chastise,* using the Upkeep 'Bouncing Bomb'[1] for which the Type 464 Provisioning modification was utilised.

There was also the enormous 'Grand Slam' weapon, a 22,000 lb (9,979.03 kg) bomb. The bomb's casing was cast from a special chrome molybdenum steel and filled with 9,975 lb (4.534 kg) of Torpex. It stood 26 ft (8 m) high and had a diameter of 5 ft (1.53 m), all of which required adaptations, modifications and even special models in order to carry such weaponry into battle. Apart from the conversions, in late 1944 a standard Newton Heath Mk I aircraft was taken from the line and customised to accommodate the 'Ten Ton Tessie' bomb. This involved, among other changes, the omitting of two of the defensive gun turrets, at the nose and dorsal locations, and

the removing of the bomb bay doors completely and cutting away parts of the aperture just to embark this fearsome object. To take the weight until the machine could become airborne, the whole undercarriage was strengthened and the airframe reinforced, and she became the prototype B Mk I ('Special'). This aircraft underwent trials from February 1945 onward, following which two orders were placed for an additional 43 such 'Specials', 32 Mk Is and eleven Mk. IIIs. They were built to tote a 12,000 lb-plus (5,443.10 kg) 'Tallboy' bomb into action, although their 'all-up' weight was duly restricted to 72,000 lbs (32,658.65 kg) and so other equipment had to be sacrificed.

Lancaster production peaked in the autumn of 1944 and by then, with the British, Canadian and American armies well into France and the Low Countries and the enormous Soviet armies bulldozing their way westward through Poland and the Balkans, the writing was clearly on the wall for the German enemy and thoughts began to turn to the Far East. Although the Lancaster had been striking to the very eastern boundaries of the Greater German Reich from her

Above left: The beautifully streamlined 12,000 lb 'Tallboy' bomb was an entirely different weapon to the 12,000 lb HC bomb that was used a year earlier.

Above right: A 'Grand Slam' in place under the belly of a Lancaster B.I Special. The metal 'strap' was installed to give the bomb extra stability during flight.

[1.] The RAF actually termed this weapon a mine, as it detonated under water, but as they were set to explode at a set depth and were spherical, it was a depth charge. The German name, *Rotations-Wasserbombe,* (Rolling Water-bomb), appears to be the most accurate description.

A 22,000 lb 'Grand Slam' sits on a bomb trolley awaiting the armourers. The Lancaster B.I Special was fitted with ribbed tyres to give it more grip on the runway at take-off. Every reserve of power and speed was needed to get the heavily laden Lancaster off the ground.

46. Plans called for some thirty Lancaster squadrons to be flown out and based as far forward as Okinawa, in the Pacific, between August and November 1945 ready to participate in softening-up raids on the Japanese home islands. The special conditions appertaining to the Pacific Theatre brought about orders for specially adapted Lancasters, the Mk. I (FE), to suit those Far East conditions and twenty-five were initially ordered as a special batch. The main Lancaster contribution was to be the new Mk. VII (FE) incorporating all the modifications, which included the new 1,640 hp Merlin 24 engine, replacing the quadruple 0.303-inch with the twin .0.5-inch Browning turret, a twin dorsal 0.5-inch turret and an extra 1,800-litre fuel tank mounted in the rear of the bomb bay which would give them an extra 1,100 km range. They were to be painted in a tropical colour scheme – white upper surfaces and black under surfaces. These 'Tiger Force' Lancasters were to be supplemented by special Lancasters equipped with lifeboats for long-distance attacks or as rescue aircraft for the aftermath of such risky raids. Those

Lincolnshire bases, the Pacific area of operations required even greater reach. The proposed 'Tiger Force' envisaged long-range missions and aerial refuelling. Specialised equipment was to be installed.

Although the war with Japan had hitherto been mainly an air-sea war dominated by carrier-borne aircraft, as the Americans closed in on the home islands thought was being given to a heavy bomber campaign on similar lines to that waged against German cities, and the RAF began to develop plans to join in prior to what were expected to be the Allied landings in Japan itself, scheduled for 1945-

that were to be retained in the Indian Ocean area to assist in the liberation of Burma and the planned liberation of Malaya were to tote both the Grand Slam and the newly-introduced 5,300 kg (11,684 lb) 'Tallboy' bombs.

The Mark.VI, only ten of which were finally constructed, were produced simply as flying test-beds for the Rolls Royce Merlin 85 and Merlin 87 engines, but they were not restricted merely to trials units and served in front line squadrons on operational missions.

The Lancaster was basically a flying bombing platform, the then ultimate expression of aviation technology and power. She represented the state-of-the-art of her day, functional, complex and typifying the sheer brute force aspect of all-out air warfare. Like a British Battleship's guns, Churchill's jaw or the White Cliffs of Dover, the "Lanc" typified British determination and resolution in adversity to the war-weary average citizen, tired of always being on the receiving end all the time in this war. When the Lancaster bomber stream filled the night-skies heading out east toward Germany it meant, as no other symbol so obviously could, that Britain was, at long last, hitting back.

Left: This newly constructed Lancaster III, PB995 is seen up on a test flight. It was the first B.I Special used for trials carrying the 12,000 lb 'Tallboy' bomb. The production aircraft had the mid-upper and nose turrets removed. This aircraft was on strength with No. 617 Squadron in early 1945, before finally being scrapped in March of 1948.

THE basic dimensions and details of the Lancaster I, III and X, which were the principal Marks used by Bomber Command, were almost identical with the main differences being the four engines with which they were equipped and the respective controls. The designed crew complement was seven which comprised the Captain-Pilot; a Second Pilot; a Navigator/Bomb-Aimer (Air Observer); two Wireless Operator/Air Gunners and two Air Gunners. All Lancasters were all-metal monoplanes, constructed in the mid-wing configuration for maximum strength.

As with most aircraft of this period, the Lancaster fuselage was built of monocoque construction, with a light alloy sheeted skin affixed by countersunk-head rivets over a framework of transverse channel-section formers braced with fore-and-aft (longitudinal) angle stringers. The large ventral opening in this box-like structure (itself slightly tapering toward the rear), which formed the large bomb/torpedo bay had its side formers made of pressed steel. The enormous bomb bay which made the Lancaster the versatile aircraft that she was, with a seemingly endless capacity to encompass larger and larger loads, was truly cavernous and stretched from beneath the pilots' seats to well aft of the trailing edges of the mainplane.

Such a (for its time) large aircraft had to be constructed in five sections, the nose, containing the front gun turret and bomb-aiming station; the front centre, which contained the twin pilot, observer, navigator and radio operator's stations; the intermediate centre, which was a rest area; the rear centre portion, mid-gun turret(s) and operational section; and rear fuselage which held the empennage including the rear gun turret. However, for transport between the various plants only four were utilised, with the nose and front centre segments bolted together as one unit (the front end).

The main plane was of cantilever construction whose horizontal centre section was uniform throughout, with the outer plane tapered with a 70 degree dihedral (+/- 15') while there was a 4 degree angle of incidence on the main plane chord line. Again, this large and complex structure was built in seven subdivisions to facilitate transport, these being the centre plane; the trailing edge, centre plane, port and starboard; the outer plane, port and starboard; the trailing edge, outer plane port and starboard; the wing tip port and starboard; the port and starboard ailerons; the pairs of flaps, two port and two starboard and the centre plane hinged leading edge, port and starboard.

The wings had the centre section of the main plane built integral with the centre fuselage section for rigidity and strength and also housed the wing fuel tanks and the housing for the engine nacelles, into the underside of which the main wheels of the aircraft's undercarriage fully retracted and thus incorporated considerable bracing and the various hydraulic systems. These included those operating the split trailing-edge flaps, which were fitted to the centre section trailing edge and the inboard end of the outer plane trailing edge. The ailerons were affixed to the outer end of the outer plane with trimming tab and balance tabs incorporated. Along the strengthened leading edge were incorporated cutters of barrage balloon cables. The wing tip extremities were of wooden construction, laminated mahogany, and contained navigation and air-to-air recognition lamps under transparent covers. With a span of 102 ft (31.09 m), the main wing area was 1,300 sq.ft (210.80 sq.m). Wing loading was 48 lb/sq.ft (240 kg/sq.m). Power/mass ratio was 0.081 hp/lb (130 w/kg).

The twin-boom type tail unit, adopted to offer a better field of defensive fire to the rear gunners, comprised a tail plane with port and starboard elevator and associated trimming and balance tabs incorporated, with the twin fins and rudders at its extremities. The tail unit was made in two sections, of the same basic construction as the

Left: This view of a Lancaster production line shows the various sections in which the aircraft was constructed.

main plane and was bolted at the centre of the fuselage. The span was 33 ft (10.06 m), and had a mean chord, including elevator of 7 ft (2.13 m) while the combined fin and rudder area was 111.40 sq.ft (10.35 sq.m).

The standard Lancaster had an overall length of 69.5 ft (21.18 m) and an overall height of 20.5 ft (6.25 m), both with tail up. She was indeed a 'heavy' with a tare weight of 36,00 lbs (16,740 kg), a loaded weight of 45,000 lbs (20,412 kg), and a gross weight of 55,000 lbs (30,840 kg). Maximum take-off weight fully armed and equipped was 72,000 lb (32,660 kg).

As we have seen, to lift this bulky monster off the ground and keep her airborne, the Mark-I was powered by the Rolls Royce Merlin XX, 22 or 24, with SU (Skinners Union) carburettors, while the –III was originally powered by the Packard-built Merlin 28 or 38, with Bendix Stromberg pressure-injection carburettors. All these in-line engines were fitted with three-bladed de Havilland 5140 or Nash Kelvinator A5/138 (some with the Rotol) variable-pitch constant speed (Hydromatic) propellers and they were fitted with two-speed superchargers. These engines were mounted on nacelles fixed to the centre and outer wing sections respectively, with their respective oil tanks carried at the rear of the nacelle and separated by a fireproof bulkhead. Only the limited run of the Mark-II was equipped with the radial-engined Bristol Hercules VI or XVI 214-cylinder, sleeve-valve, air-cooled, each of which was rated at 1,735 hp, and there were a few other experimental exceptions. Oil capacity was 100 Imp. Gal. (455 litres) per engine.

This power plant and fuel capacity gave the Lancaster a maximum range of 2,700 nautical miles (3,000 miles or 4,600 km) with a minimum bomb load, and a service ceiling of 23,500 ft (7,160 m). The flying statistics for a normally equipped Lancaster were relatively mundane of course – she was a load-carrying workhorse, not a racehorse (one famous test pilot, Alex Henshaw, actually barrel-rolled a Lancaster bomber, but it was not generally recommended!) Her efficiency was rated on the amount of destructive firepower she could carry and how far into the heart of Germany she could deliver it. Thus, with engines generating 3000 rpm (on rich mixture) and at 9.0 Pressure Indication Switch (PIS) Boost, maximum speed at 12,800 ft (3,904 m) was a stately 261 mph (420 km/h). Her economical cruising speed was 239 mph (385 km/h) at 14,600 ft (4,450m), and she had a stalling speed of 95 mph (153 km/h) with flaps up or 80

mph (129 km/h) with flaps and undercarriage lowered. To get off the ground the Lancaster required 1,550 yds (1,420 m) of runway, and, once she was airborne she took 41.6 minutes to ponderously climb to 20,000 ft (6,100 m), a rate of climb of 250 ft (76 m) per minute. Maximum operational ceiling was listed as 24,400 ft (7,437 m).

The six wing-mounted, self-sealing fuel tanks were positioned to port (left) and starboard (right) outboard from the fuselage and identified as No.1 (or Inner), of 580 Imp. Gal. (2,637 litres) capacity, located between the fuselage and the inner engine; No. 2 (or centre), of 383-gallon (1,741 litres) capacity, between the inner and outer engines and No. 3 (or outer) containing 114 gallons (518 litres), outboard of the outer engine, giving a total 2,154 Imp. Gal. (9,792 litres) – 1,077 gallons (4,896 litres) in either wing. Provision could also be built in to selected equipped machines to carry either one or a pair of additional fuel tanks of 400 gallons (1,820 litres) capacity in the bomb cells, and these transferred their fuel to the engine via No. 1 tank. These tanks proved highly vulnerable to night fighter attacks from below and, in March 1944, led to the introduction of the installation of an in-tank nitrogen system to lessen the risk of combustion.

The aircrew accommodation from nose to tail was designed for seven personnel, although various mission configurations saw considerable leeway above and below this datum, with extra crew or observers being embarked for some missions, while, conversely, extra heavy ordnance requirements would see various aircrew omitted for obvious weight-saving requirements. From nose to tail this layout encompassed the following positions and equipments.

Ahead of the main cockpit, the nose section extended forward and consisted of a bulbous transparent lower section, with a flat section of perspex inset in the bottom half in order to provide a clear, distortion-free viewing panel for the prone air-bomber (bomb-aimer). A hand-operated glycol de-icing pump and reservoir was a necessary piece of equipment and usually an F24 adjustable ventral camera was carried on the port side forward. The floor was fitted with instrumental aids to bombing and target location, principally a Mk. II or Mk. XIV automatic bomb sight and associated computer, both bomb sight and steering control panels, a height and speed computer, a target map case, an automatic bomb distributor, with a Connell Pre-selector and bomb selector, fusing switches and the

Above: A close-up of the Fraser Nash FN5 nose turret and shallow bomb-aimer's blister as fitted to Manchesters and early mark Lancasters.

Above: The Lancaster effectively used the Manchester fuselage. The forward turret and bomb-aimer's blister were identical. Though the blister was enlarged on later mark Lancasters.

A bomb aimer sitting at a Mark XIV bomb sight which was standard equipment for most Lancasters of RAF Bomber Command. It was introduced into RAF service in 1942 and was designed for area bombing. It was also known as the "Blackett bomb sight" after Patrick Blackett who invented it.

bomb release gear. The Mark IX Course-Setting Bomb Sight (CSBS) featured manual pre-setting but was found inflexible and soon ditched. On later aircraft, electronic gyros replaced the pneumatic gyro drives in the American-built T1 version of the Mark XIV, while for highly-specialised missions the famous No. 617 Squadron utilised the tachometric Stabilizing Automatic Bomb Sight (SBAS). The limited floor area was fitted with soft kneeling pads along with adjustable supporting handles and grips for the air-bomber to sight from a prone or semi-prone position as the target was approached. Set above the air-bomber's restricted space, the hydraulically-operated FN5 nose turret was positioned on its support ring.

The heart of the Lancaster was the front centre portion, which contained the dual pilot (fixed) and flight engineer's (hinged) cockpit seats, along with their associated instrument panels, the air-observer's station, the wireless operator's station and the fighting control station. This vital area was protected by steel plates and a bullet proof glass screen. Along the starboard side was a communal fore-and-aft gangway allowing all positions, including the nose, to be accessed by the various crew members.

The pilot himself, no matter what his rank, was always the aircraft captain. He was assisted by the flight engineer, especially with the throttle controls on the take-off and landings. He was sufficiently proficient to take over the controls in 'straight-and-level' flight but his main duties were to monitor essential oil and fuel levels and pressures, and similar monitoring. The flying controls were conventional for their day; rudder control was via pendulum rudder pedals, with a hand-wheel control column for ailerons and elevators, which worked tubular push-pull connectors, save for the chain, tie-rod and cable for the aileron controls.

Behind the pilot's seating was the air-observer/navigator's curtained-off kingdom, with the navigation table and the hinged instruments panel ranged along the port side. Chart stowage, a flexible lamp, sextant, torch, Aldis signalling lamp, fire extinguisher, code books, and other sundry equipments were stowed here. The observation instrument panel similarly disposed to starboard and both were served by a single swivelling seat. At the top rear end of the canopy was a perspex observation dome (astrodome) for star shots. As new instrumentation was developed as the campaign went on, the navigator's duties became ever more complex, but remained, in essence, the plotting of the course to and from the target, watching

When in flight the Flight Engineer had the option of a fold-down seat although many rarely used it. The thin cables in the canopy roof are there for sun shades which could be pulled forward to alleviate glare.

the wind variations and keeping the aircraft on track. It was a constant job allowing for little relaxation.

Next came the radio station, with the forward facing wireless operator's seat. The bulky radio equipment comprised either a remotely-controlled T.R. 9F or a T.R.1196 pilot's set, while the navigator's T.R. 1335 set was stacked on and below a traverse-mounted table with amplifying gear, a crystal monitor, the

The pilot had a large piece of armour plating fitted behind his head as protection from an attack from the rear.

distribution panel for the mic-tel (intercom), and a winch aerial, which could be cranked down and accessed from here via a sliding panel. At the rear end the Direction Finding loop was affixed to the top canopy. There was also the wireless operator's T.1154-R.1155 set, (although many Canadian-built machines had alternative American sets) while IFF R.3003 or R.3090 (Identification Friend or Foe) Transponders, and Beam approach with T.3135/R.3136 equipment. The radio operator was also expected to have a minimum knowledge of the navigator's trade in case the latter was incapacitated, and to be a first aid specialist.

Abaft this nerve centre, split into two sections separated by a bulkhead of armoured plate which was pierced by two doors, lay the intermediate centre portion. For crew purposes the rear compartment was used as a rest area as well as oxygen bottle and parachute storage and an emergency exit via the roof.

Next in line was the rear centre portion, which housed mid-upper FN50 and (originally) the aft-facing lower FN64 mid gun turrets. Here also was located another emergency exit, and both spare and rear gun supply ammunition stowage boxes, the latter feeding aft to the rear gun position on tracking. A reconnaissance flare station was also located here along both walls with release chute at the end.

Finally the rear fuselage held, at its extremity and fearfully isolated, the rear rotating FN20 or, later, FN121 gun turret, accessed by way of a door on the starboard bulkhead. To reach it one had to edge

Behind the navigator facing forward was the Wireless Operator. Sitting next to the cabin heating outlet, the W/Ops could always be spotted on crew photographs as he always wore the least amount of flying clothing!

Left: The navigator sat sideways behind the pilot. Seen here is Flying Officer Ingleby of No. 619 Squadron.

through the compartment – which contained the Directional Rotating compass, a dozen vacuum flasks, further parachutes and a trio of marine distress signals, first aid equipment and the like, as well as the Elsan sanitary toilet – and use the toilet lid itself as a means of stepping up to a narrow walkway with handrails. The main inward-opening entrance door for the entire aircrew was located just ahead of the tailplane, on the starboard side, along with a hooked access ladder. The track carrying the 10,000 rounds of 0.303 bullets from their four storage boxes ran aft here with the gunner's own parachute stowage.

The rear gunner of a Lancaster was not a man to be envied. Being 'Tail-end Charlie' not only meant being of small stature, but also possessing a stoical if not fatalistic nature, for nobody was more isolated and cut off from human contact than the rear gunner during the cold (in some cases temperatures as low as –40 degrees), long and dangerous hours as they fought their way to the target and back again in the darkness. The frosting-up of the flexi-glass centre panel, the

gunner's principal viewing area, led to some of them physically removing it in order to guarantee a vital unrestricted view to ensure survival, no matter what the cost physically. As the majority of German night fighters attacked from astern and had the elimination of the rear gunner as their number one priority, the vulnerability of these gunners was absolute. No air gunner's job was a sinecure of course and some 20,000 were killed during the war, but the rear gunner's job was especially dangerous. Let this memoir by Canadian Clayton Moore give some indication of what it was like:

"As we droned out over the Channel, the silence of the intercom was occasionally interrupted by the quiet, business-like report of a crew member. 'Levelling out at twenty thousand feet', Then, 'We should be crossing the enemy coast in five minutes, and the Gee's packed up, skipper.' This didn't mean that Gee, the navigational aid, had developed a fault, but that the Jerries were jamming it. It also meant that navigation from this point on would depend entirely on the expertise of Dick Lodge as he sat out the trip in his tiny, curtained and dimly-lit 'office', sandwiched between the flight deck and the wireless operator's compartment. Immediately aft of the latter crew position was the sturdy armour-plated bulkhead, the door of which was always kept tightly closed in order to provide protection for the forward crew members from the danger that a fighter attack from the rear would produce. The presence of this bulkhead and its ever-closed door came to represent something of a symbol of us gunners from our comrades at arms. To Dick and me, it symbolised the dividing line between companionship and isolation; protection and exposure; aggression and defence – even between comfort and discomfort, since there was no heating in our dark and inhospitable domain."

The mid-upper gunner had a 360 degree field of view. His guns were automatically restricted by a taboo track to stop him shooting at the extremities of his own aircraft.

He continued:

"The long hours spent in searching the surrounding gloom for lurking shadows could be almost unbearably monotonous at times, and the sound of a voice was all that was needed to ease the feeling of total isolation and loneliness that was so much a part of the tail gunner's lot. From my perspex capsule at the extreme end of the aircraft, there was little to be seen except the receding hostile sky from which I was being transported by the almost invisible platform I was riding. The mid-upper turret commanded a plan view of the complete Lancaster, but I could only see a small part of the tailplane on either side of my position."[1]

Harold Clark, of Nova Scotia, served as a tail gunner with No. 443, Porcupine Squadron, RCAF. He informed the Nanton Lancaster Society that with regard to the tail gunner's parachute, it was impossible to actually wear it, but that it "was placed just in the back of the aircraft, close to the turret. It was impossible to put on without exiting from the turret." His solution was a seat chute.

Although a gunner, the principal duty of the man in the rear turret was airborne sentinel, watching the dark sky for the blur that

[1] Clayton Moore, *Lancaster Valour: The Valour and The Truth*, Compaid Graphics, Warrington, 1995.

Flt.Lt. J. A. Howard, DFC, sits snugly in his Lancaster's FN20 rear turret.

Far right: A view of the entrance and interior of a Lancaster's FN20 rear turret.

meant an incoming attacker, and the survival of the aircraft and his six companions often rested on his alertness – despite the cold at 20,000 feet, which often meant temperatures of below freezing.

The myriad of electrical wiring, switching and fusing was serviced via a service panel located ahead of the front spar on the starboard side. The basic electrical installation for the Lancaster was a 24-volt, 80-Ah system fed from the two 1.500-watt generators in conjunction with a quartet of 12-volt, 40-Ah accumulators.

Not surprisingly, the undercarriage and associated hydraulic gear for the Lancaster was a formidable assembly for its day.

Each of the main wheel units, which fully retracted into its own compartment in the engine nacelle, had the individual tyre and wheel axle 'bookended' by a pair of shock absorber struts, which were held in place by bracing tubes. The whole shock absorber strut was hinged to a folding bracket fixed to the rear end of the mainplane rear spar. Standard Dowty oleo-pneumatic shock absorbers were fitted with an unloaded air pressure of 995 lb/sq.in (457.32 kg/sq/m) and the

whole tyre unit retracted upward and backward towards the rear of the aircraft by means of hydraulic jacking; the fairing doors automatically closed. The smaller rear tail wheel was a fixed structure, fully castoring, which also featured Dowty oleo-pneumatic and self-centring, affixed to the rear fuselage with a plug and sleeve. The undercarriage lever was cockpit located, with a locking bolt to prevent accidental retraction and green light indication lamps for 'lock-down' and red for 'unlocked'. There was also an emergency lowering system worked by compressed air.

The main wheel tyres were Dunlop SK.A. 64, 24 inch x 19 inch, (60.96 cm x 48.26 cm) having 43 lb/sq.in (19.50 kg/m) working

Right: The arrowhead 'Monica' aerial clearly visible under the rear turret. Note the gunner has removed some of the turret's perspex to give him clearer vision and it was found that the difference in temperature inside was minimal.

Left: A direct rear view of Flt.Lt. J. A. Howard, DFC, in a standard FN 20 rear turret. Armament was 4 x .303 inch Browning machine guns. Typically, the central perspex panel has been removed to improve the rear gunner's view.

very tough bird, these added considerably to the rate of loss, which was already high during the winters of 1943/44 and 1944/45. At one time, indeed, the numbers of damaged and written-off Lancasters became so high that Churchill was forced to memo Arthur Harris, reminding him that, great though the need was to continue the offensive to the limits of the possible, he was not expecting him to fight the weather as well as the Germans!

The hydraulically-operated Nash & Thomson gun turrets which formed the Lancaster's defence against German interceptors are deserving of greater study. It had become a widely-held belief that the provision of large numbers of gun positions would make the heavy bomber too prickly a target for the lightly-armed biplane fighter aircraft of the 1930s to tackle and that, given sufficient gun turrets, the heavy bomber would be able to shrug off any such attacks. Such a belief was not just confined to the Royal Air Force; all nations followed it, and such notions were part of the *raison d'être* of the American B-17 Flying Fortress, for example, whose very name epitomised the concept.

An enormous amount of expertise was thrown into these defensive turrets and, in Great Britain, two main designers dominated – Boulton Paul and Nash & Thomson. The well known Boulton Paul designs were in fact licensed from the French specialist company SAMM. SAMM became a subsidiary of the PSA Peugeot Citroen group and French engineer, J.B.A. De Boysson, had at an early stage developed a 4-gun electro-hydraulic turret. John North of Boulton & Paul, realising its value, had purchased the manufacturing rights and developed it further. Their designs used individual pumps integral to each turret and utilised the 24-volt system to power their products. As well as equipping failed fighter aircraft designs such as the Boulton & Paul Defiant and the Blackburn Roc, their products were mainly used more successfully on the contemporary Handley-Page Halifax heavy bomber.

The contemporaneous development by the British innovator Archibald Frazer-Nash, had led to the establishment, with Henry R Godfrey in 1929, of the Kingston-upon-Thames company of Nash & Thomson in order to develop and produce these weapons. Frazer-Nash's (FN) fully-enclosed gun turrets, with hydraulic transmission, and 300 lb p.s.i. operating pressure, featured the remotely-powered concept and much later he became involved in the production of similarly powered radar scanners, like the A1 Mark VIII and H2S. The

pressure, equipped with Dunlop pneumatic AH.8039 brakes with 80 lb/sq.in (36.287 kg/m) working pressure; while the tail wheel tyre was a Dunlop NX.30, 12.5 inch x 120 inch (31.75 cm x 305 cm)) with 54 lb/sq.in (24.49 kg/m) pressure. The main undercarriage wheel track was 23 ft 9 in (723.9 cm).

Wheels-up landings were frequent, due to both enemy action damage and bad weather accidents and although the Lancaster was a

Left and above: The rear Rose turret incorporated two heavier calibre 0.5 inch Browning machine guns, with three hundred and fifty rounds per gun, with an effective range of six hundred and fifty yards. The heavy guns were for daylight use, since limited visibility at night made their longer range ineffective compared to the more rapid fire of the lighter .303 Brownings. It used a Barr & Stroud Mk IIIA reflector sight with a traverse of +/- 94 degrees, elevation 49 degrees and a depression of 59 degrees and allowed for a total firing time of around 24 seconds compared with the 130 seconds firing time for the four-gun Frazer-Nash turret. They were fitted to around 400 Lancasters and, in many ways, were a great improvement in fire power. They were also easier for the gunner to leave in an emergency, allowing him to wear a back type parachute.

The 'Village Inn' gunlaying radar, with the scanner dome fitted below the rear turret of a Lancaster, allowed the rear gunner to engage targets on radar indications alone. Operated in the blind firing mode, it could have made life extremely uncomfortable for the Luftwaffe's night-fighter crews, but problems in producing and installing the infrared lights in the nose of each bomber to identify them as friendly could not be resolved before the war ended. As a result, 'Village Inn' could not be used to its full capability.

Another view of a Lancaster fitted with the Automatic Gunlaying Turret (AGLT) radar known as 'Village Inn'. By the time of Germany's surrender it however had only been installed in a limited number of aircraft so that its use in combat made no difference to the overall outcome of the bomber offensive.

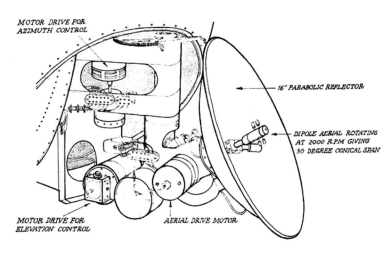

MOTOR DRIVE FOR AZIMUTH CONTROL

16" PARABOLIC REFLECTOR

DIPOLE AERIAL ROTATING AT 2000 R.P.M GIVING 30 DEGREE CONICAL SPAN

MOTOR DRIVE FOR ELEVATION CONTROL

AERIAL DRIVE MOTOR

A diagram showing the main components of the 'Village Inn' scanning system.

turrets, both two-and four-gun versions, principally were designed to accommodate the British Vickers K or the American Browning machine gun of 0.303-inch (7.7-mm) calibre. Eventually a range of 20 or more marks of gun turret were developed of which eight, the FN5, FN20, FN50, FN64, FN82, FN120, FN121 and FN150, were fitted to some degree to the Lancaster bomber. Despite the inadequacy of the 0.303 against German night fighters equipped with cannon, the Air Ministry was slow in introducing a more powerful turret. It was only on the initiative of the Air Officer Commanding No. 1 Group, Air Vice Marshal Sir Edward Rice, who had informal talks with the chief of Rose Brothers, a Gainsborough-based engineering company, that the Rose-Rice turret was developed at all, the Air Ministry ordering some in June 1943. This tail turret bore a twin 0.50 Browning but was only carried by the ten squadrons of 1 Group Lancasters. From combat experience it seems as if the chief advantage of this turret was not so much heavier firepower as much better visibility, which resulted in a greater chance of spotting and thereby avoiding, by 'corkscrewing' or other evasive tactics, being attacked at all!

The Frazer-Nash 0.5-inch tail turrets, which found greater favour, were the FN82 and the later FN120/121, but again, they were installed only in a few Lancasters prior to the war's termination. Frazer-Nash's turrets were also fitted to the Armstrong-Whitworth Whitley, Vickers Wellington, Blackburn Botha, Short Stirling, Short Sunderland and other bombing types and the mushrooming demand led to subcontracting of the product, much by the Parnall Aircraft Company.

The faith placed in the multiple machine gun to defend bombers very quickly evaporated in the harsh reality of war, however. Heavy losses to German fighter aircraft forced the RAF to switch to night attacks. Even so, the multiple turret had to be retained as night fighters quickly developed, but more and more the chief role of the turret gunners became aerial lookout – with early warning of attacks vital for the pilot to put into practice the evasive 'corkscrew' manoeuvre to evade destruction. An accurate burst of fire, and the occasional 'kill', were morale-boosting events, but mainly they persuaded experienced German fighter pilots to break off an attack and seek less alert prey – from which, of course, they had hundreds to choose on any one night.

The punching power of the 0.303 was also found wanting: formidable as it had seemed in the mid-1930s, the German night fighters of a decade later were able to absorb such small-calibre ordnance pretty well and were able to stay out of range and hack into the bombers with their 20-mm (0.75-inch) cannon with relative impunity. Nonetheless, the Royal Canadian Air Force at least realised that something better in the way of deterrent firepower was required and began to switch over to the more lethal Martin 250 CE turret, carrying a pair of 0.50-calibre machine guns already being toted by such USAAF bombers as the Douglas A-20 Havoc, the Consolidated B-24 Liberator, the Martin B-26 Marauder and the Boeing B-17 Flying Fortress. Some 276 of the 431 Canadian-built Lancasters embarked this weapon in lieu of the Frazer-Nash for their mid-upper defences. However, very few of these aircraft had actually taken this weapon into combat over the shrinking skies of Germany from the time they were introduced.

The majority of British-built Lancasters finally had their defences concentrated upon just three Frazer-Nash turrets: the FN5 twin-gun nose turret; the FN50 twin-gun mid-upper turret; and the FN20 or FN121 quadruple turret. Many held that this was an inadequate number, although the dropping of the mid-low FN64 periscope-sighted twin ventral turret was the result of war experience which seemed to indicate that it was inefficient and had little or no fighting value. A few aircraft unofficially fitted a single 0.50-calibre machine gun instead, but the arrival of the H2S radar unit finally filled this void much more effectively, as we shall see.

Of the three turrets, the bomb-aimer's FN5 nose turret was probably the least used in combat. The whole concept of German night interception attacks was based on achieving surprise; head-on attacks were not a frequent occurrence and therefore the nose defence was not often called into action. The field of fire had an azimuth[2] of 184 degrees, a maximum elevation of 60 degrees and a maximum depression of 45 degrees. Like the other turrets, this weapon was fitted with the Palmer Hydraulic firing control mechanism and a free gun reflector sight, various marks of which were in use – Mk.III, Mk. IIIA, Mk. IIIN and, for the FN121, the Gyro Gun Sight (GGS) Mk IIC, invented by Maurice Hancock of the Royal Aircraft Establishment (RAE) Farnborough, and developed with Bernard Wheeler Robinson and Ben Sykes.

The mid-upper turret gunner had a good all-round view above, astern and ahead, and was also the best-placed person to check on damage received from either fighter attack or anti-aircraft bursts. A few fatal accidents led to the introduction of safety-stops on the after fire sectors on this turret to prevent the gunner from accidentally shooting off portions of his own aircraft's empennage in the heat of action, but this did not restrict observation.

The heaviest punch was, as we have seen, reserved for the rear gunner, whose quadruple Brownings were considered the first line of defence. The azimuth was 168 degrees, elevation 60 degrees and depression, 45 degrees. Chances of survival were slim, for he was unable to wear his parachute. The only way to abandon this position if the aircraft was fatally damaged was to open the rear doors, grab his parachute and harness, somehow clip it safely to his body, then rotate the turret a full 90 degrees and eject himself rearward on his back. One consolation, should he achieve all this in the brief time left to him, was that there were no obstructions to his departure.

This then, was essentially the Avro Lancaster, in which the Royal Air Force's Bomber Command had a remarkably efficient, rugged and durable weapon, capable of carrying the heaviest mix of ordnance into the heart of the Reich. Finally the Air Marshals had the aircraft they had long desired to do the job that they had convinced themselves would transform warfare, all warfare, totally. Let us turn to examine how the brave young men who flew her and the Lancaster herself, set about this remarkable mission.

Post-war use of the 'Village Inn' AGLT continued with its fitment into the FN82 rear turret of an Avro Lincoln. The Lincoln was a development of the Lancaster.

2. Azimuth - the vertical arc of sky from zenith to horizon.

A brand new Lancaster awaits
delivery. The paddle blade props
can be seen very clearly in this
photograph.

4 Combat and Evolution

The basic weapons platform was impressive enough and the new 'heavy' was soon to become the mainstay of Bomber Command's widening offensive. However, impressive though the expansion was, the development of strategic bombing led to new target scenarios and, in turn, new ordnance. The Lancaster proved herself versatile enough to encompass all manner of adaptations and modifications to meet these fresh challenges.

Left: A Lancaster is silhouetted over Hamburg amid fires and anti-aircraft tracer on 30 January 1943. It was under these sort of conditions that the Luftwaffe developed 'Wilde Sau', (Wild Boar) which came about due to the RAF using Window (which was a radar countermeasure in which Bomber Command aircraft released a cloud of small, thin aluminium strips effectively knocking out the German Himmelbett radar defence system). 'Wild Boar' were simply single-engined day fighters ranging over German cities. The view seen by a 'Wild Boar' pilot targeting a British bomber, would have been very similar to the image opposite. This form of German air defence needed ideal conditions for its success.

THE four Lancasters that took part in that very first minelaying ('Gardening') mission in the vicinity of Heligoland on the night of 3/4 March 1942, were but the heralds of what was soon to become a deluge of Lancasters which took the war to the very heart of the German homeland. A mere trickle, then as the bombers came off the production lines in increasing numbers, fresh squadrons formed and the weight of attack increased remorselessly. Throughout 1942 numbers fluctuated but remained relatively modest; for example only two of a force of 126 heavy bombers which raided Essen on the night of 10/11 March were Lancasters and this increased to just seven from a force of 254 bombers which sortied against the same target on 25/26 March. Against the same target on 10/11 April, eight Lancasters participated, while just seven took part in an attack on Hamburg on 8/9 April. Two further minelaying missions intervened involving a mere handful of Lancasters, but these were the last of such peripheral operations.

On 17 April, Augsburg in the south of Germany was the target with 12 Lancasters, six from each of the only two operational units, Nos. 44 and 97 Squadrons, being despatched on their own in broad daylight. This proved over-confident and the result was a disastrous one, which for any other aircraft might have shaken confidence completely, for only five machines survived. The target was an important one, the *Maschinenfabrik Augsburg Nürnburg* (MAN) plant manufacturing vital diesel engines for U-boats, hence the need for precision. In order to hopefully minimise their exposure the attack was to take place just before dusk, thus, in theory, giving sufficient visibility to hit the small

Squadron Leader John Nettleton, VC, led the daring raid on Augsburg in April 1942.

target, but offering the shield of darkness for the long homeward haul. The two squadrons, spaced some two miles (3.5 km) away from each other, fielded six aircraft each, flying in four separate 'vics' of three.

Unfortunately for No. 44 Squadron, diversionary attacks planned to keep the enemy fighters engaged elsewhere had the opposite effect, and stirred up a hornet's nest right in the path of the Lancasters. Four of the six heavy bombers were destroyed in a half-hour slaughter before the Germans were forced to break off through lack of fuel. The remaining pair of Lancasters, led by South African Squadron Leader John Nettleton, bravely continued to the target and each dropped their four 1,000 lb (453.59 kg) bombs at the very low height of fifty feet (15 m), but the other Lancaster, that flown by Flying Officer R J Garwell, was then destroyed by anti-aircraft fire, leaving Nettleton as the sole survivor, for which he received the Victoria Cross. No. 97 Squadron fared slightly better, all making it through to the target, attacking from 400 ft (122 m) altitude but again, defensive flak was intense and accurate and two more of the big bombers fell victim to it, while others were hit and damaged.

Although the mission was broadcast as a successful one, actual damage was light and even Harris was forced to admit that mounting raids of this type, save when considered absolutely essential, was impractical. Again Bomber Command had re-learnt an old lesson: they were not yet a daylight precision force. Nor, with the massive expansion planned, were they ever likely to be except in a few special cases, although the introduction of new equipment was hoped to help rectify this. However, the bulk of Bomber Command essentially resigned itself to night operations and used specialist highly-trained aircrews, known as 'Pathfinders', to locate the target cities and guide the bomber streams in with green, red and yellow Target Indicators (TIs) and various coloured sky marking flares. Each type of Bomber Command aircraft had an experienced representative in the new force, and the first Lancaster Pathfinder unit was No. 83 Squadron.

The introduction of the 'Gee' receiver helped, as this was able to pick up synchronised and timed pulse signals transmitted from England. This device had a working range of 300-plus miles(483 km) and the Lancaster could work out her true position from the gaps. Not all the 'advances' proved to be advantageous once the enemy got the measure of them; some, indeed, proved lethal to the aircraft equipped with them rather than be helpful.

Typical of the latter is the notorious 'Monica' radar system. This was a 300 MHz system introduced early in 1942 to provide early warning on a rearward approach by German night fighters, and was intended to be a more reliable replacement for the weary rear gunner's 'Mark One Eyeball'. Unfortunately it promised more than it could deliver, for it could not detect an approach from underneath the aircraft, and was unable to distinguish between an incoming Me 110 or Ju 88 and another Lancaster of the bomber stream and so was virtually unusable. More serious than that was the fact that German scientists were soon able to recover such sets from the myriad of crashed bombers and analyse them, and their cavity magnetron transmissions signals. They then equipped the intercepting fighters with the Telefunken FuG 202 SN2 *Lichtenstein* airborne radar antenna. Their *Naxos Z* detectors were activated accordingly and, in conjunction with their obliquely-mounted *Schräge Musik* (Jazz) cannon, the defenders could easily home on to any Lancaster which had its 'Monica' activated. It took the lucky capture of a German night fighter before this was realised and 'Monica' was promptly abandoned for RAF aircraft.

The H2S navigation radar was a 10-cm/3 GHz ground-searching system in its function, and was able to differentiate between built-up areas and water. It could 'see' through clouds and so bad weather as such was not a deterrent, nor was the routine black-out of all lights in the target area; H2S was all-seeing. It was put into good effect with the 25 July attack on Hamburg, along with the dropping of 'Window', a mass of thin aluminium strips, blackened on one side and tied into bundles. These bundles were hand-fed into one of the

Air Chief Marshal Sir Arthur Harris, KCB OBE AFC. 'Bomber Harris' was in command of RAF Bomber Command from 22 February 1942 until his retirement in September 1945.

flare discharge chutes at the rate of one per minute. As this cloud of foil strips fluttered to earth, they reflected back radar pulses and totally confused the German defences. Three subsequent heavy attacks followed on the same city, which saw massive collateral damage and enormous civilian casualties.

H2S, although initially a boon, also later became vulnerable to the German Telefunken-built FuG 350 (*Naxos*[1]) airborne radar detector and required careful usage. The 'Fishpond' device was added later which gave a supplementary ventral coverage to the main; while

---

[1]. The Germans code-named their various detectors after islands; Flensburg, Korfu etc. This device was named after one in the Aegean.

This Lancaster B.I, RA530, DX-Y, has a red vertical bar painted on its fin with the red, white and blue flash having been deleted. This aircraft joined No. 57 Squadron in February 1945 and was destroyed in a crash at Stockley village, just after taking off for a raid on Böhlen near Leipzig on 20/21 March 1945. The H2S radar scanner was housed under the rear fuselage in a teardrop-shaped blister. The rear of the blister was left unpainted to allow the downward recognition lights to be seen.

the 'Boozer' system could detect when the Lancaster was being homed in on by either airborne or ground systems, and warn the aircrew by illuminating lights on the aircraft's instrument panel. Again, these lights proved over-sensitive, their reaction causing many false alerts and alarms that tended to discount their usefulness by crying 'wolf' too often!

On the night of 30/31 May 1942, Harris managed to scrape together sufficient bombers of all types (and from all commands) and launched a long-awaited attack, the first of the 'Thousand Bomber Raids', Operation *Millennium,* with Cologne as the target. By ruthlessly stripping the training units of instructors and even trainee pilots, sufficient aircraft were assembled and organised. In all, among the Halifaxes, Stirlings and six hundred Vickers Wellingtons which made up that force of 1,047 heavy bombers, flying from 53 British aerodromes that night, were seventy-three Lancasters, all from No. 5 Group, and only one was lost.

As well as a masterful demonstration of improvisation, *Millennium* introduced for the first time the concept of the 'Bomber Stream', whereby an enormous number of heavy bombers could be channelled into a funnel of similar height and time. Such a force would totally swamp the relatively thin defences of *Luftwaffe* radar sites, flak guns and fighter controllers, (who were only able to direct six interceptions in any hour at this stage of the war) as well as the German civil defences. Commencing at 00.47 on the morning of 31 May, the RAF planned that *every one* of the 868 bombers allocated against the main target itself, would pass through a one-and-a-half hour window over the city. The risk of in-air collisions was accepted, and, in fact, proved minimal.

The result was devastating. Some 1,455 tons (1,478,348 kg) of bombs were dropped and, of these, two-thirds were incendiaries which ignited no fewer than 2,500 different fires, 1,700 of them 'large' by German fire brigade classification. These fires did far more

Continued on page 60

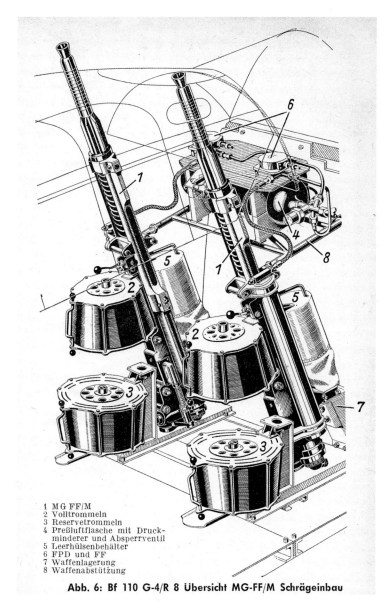

1 MG FF/M
2 Volltrommeln
3 Reservetrommeln
4 Preßluftflasche mit Druck-
  minderer und Absperrventil
5 Leerhülsenbehälter
6 FPD und FF
7 Waffenlagerung
8 Waffenabstützung

Abb. 6: Bf 110 G-4/R 8 Übersicht MG-FF/M Schrägeinbau

Above: The 'Schräge Musik' upward-firing cannon installation with two Oerlikon MG/FF 20mm cannon, as fitted to a Messerschmitt Bf 110 G-4/R8 night fighter. These weapons fired non-tracer ammunition, which enabled the Luftwaffe to keep the weapon installation secret for several months after its operational debut.

Left: The RAF discovered the secret of the German 'Schräge Musik' upward-firing cannon after examining bombers that had survived attacks with this weapon. Steel rods show the angle of penetration - this Lancaster was lucky as the inner wing fuel tanks had not been hit.

Below: Alongside the Bf 110, the other main Luftwaffe night fighter operating against Bomber Command was the Junkers Ju 88. This Ju 88 G-7 of NJG./ 2 has alongside its belly mounted cannon, 'Schräge Musik' installed - in this case comprising MG 151 20mm.

The effective 'Corkscrew' evasive manoeuvre, employed by RAF bombers to shake off an attacking night fighter.

On detecting an enemy fighter, the bomber entered a steep diving turn to port or starboard into the direction of the attack (to port in this example), at an angle of bank 45 degrees, (**1**). This enabled the bomber to build up speed quickly, and make visual sighting from the fighter difficult since it placed the bomber beneath its level. After a descent through about 1,000 feet, the bomber reached a speed around 300 mph. Then maintaining its turn to port, it pulled up and climbed (**2**) for 4 seconds. It then rolled to starboard, and turned in that direction and continued climbing (**3**) for 4 seconds gaining 200 feet in altitude during which its speed fell to about 255 mph. The bomber then rolled into a climbing turn to starboard and speed continued to fall to about 250 mph. If the enemy fighter was still behind, there was a good chance it might overshoot the bomber. At the top of the climb the nose was pushed down again (**4**), and after a descent of 1,000 feet the turn was reversed (**5**). The bomber continued its descent through a further 1,000 feet (**6**). It then repeated the procedure from (**2**), if the fighter remained a threat. As a tactical evasive manoeuvre, the corkscrew had three outstanding features: first it gave a good chance of throwing off a nightfighter; secondly, even if it did not throw off the night fighter, the latter was left with a difficult target with almost continual and changing height and deflection with fully alert rear gunners; and thirdly, since the manoeuvre could be flown along a mean heading and height, it combined the maximum possible evasion with minimum deviation from the bomber's intended track and altitude.

A pair of Bf 110 night fighters of 9./NJG 3 on a daylight sortie in 1943 where they proved quite vunerable away from the cover of darkness to Allied fighters. These aircraft are fitted with Lichtenstein radar.

A H2S-equipped Lancaster, PA238, SR-Z, of No. 101 Squadron seen taking off from Pomigliano in Italy during 'Operation Dodge'. This was an operation where the 8th Army was brought back to the UK by holding units in Italy at the war's end. This Lancaster joined the squadron on 14 February 1945, went to 38 MU in February 1946 and was SOC in September 1947.

damage than the high-explosives, and it was estimated that nine hospitals, seventeen churches, sixteen schools, four university buildings, ten historically important buildings, two newspaper offices, four hotels, two cinemas, six department stores and twenty-one important public buildings were destroyed, in addition to 12,840 buildings of all types, including 13,010 civilian homes eliminated with another 6,360 badly damaged. Remarkably, only 486 people were killed, mostly civilians, with another 5,027 injured. This enormous damage was achieved at a cost to the RAF of just forty-three aircraft, only 3.9 per cent of the attacking force, which was less than half the one hundred machines that Churchill had told Harris he would find acceptable. It seemed to both men a very small price to pay for the elimination of Germany's third largest city.

More importantly, as far as Bomber Command was concerned, this raid, was enthusiastically embraced by both the Premier and the British public alike, (although with some notable reservations elsewhere), and thus certainly ensured the continuing strengthening of the force and strong backing for its committed policy. As Air Marshal Sir Robert Saundby enthused, Churchill was won over, "…his powerful support thereafter never wavered." He added, "The opponents of the policy of air bombardment of Germany were silenced, and enthusiasm for it was rekindled in many quarters in which it had become lukewarm."[2]

Two more 'Thousand Bomber' raids followed, with 956 bombers being sent against Essen on the night of 1/2 June 1942, of which 74 were Lancasters; and 1,067 against Bremen on the night of 25/26 June, where 96 Lancasters swelled the total. This was to be the picture as the year progressed and more and more Lancasters came 'on-stream'.

[2] Air Marshal Sir Robert Saundby, *Air Bombardment: The Story of its Development*, Chatto & Windus, London, 1961, pp141.

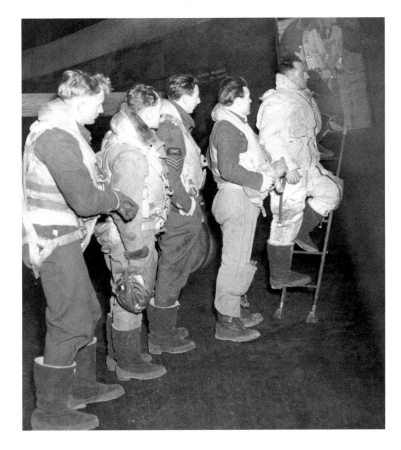

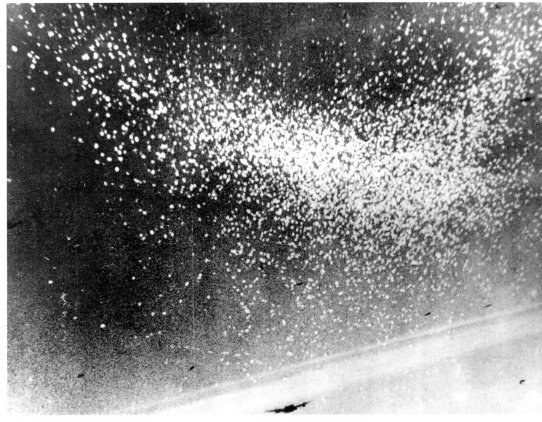

A crew board their Lancaster at the start of a mission. The gunners are the two wearing twice as much flight clothing as the others!

Top right: A cloud of Window (radar countermeasure) goes down over Essen on 11 March 1945.

Another new factor in the way in which the Lancasters were operated was the 'Shuttle' attack whereby a force was sent to attack a German target, and then, instead of a return journey back to its home bases having to avoid a fully alert enemy, it would fly on to friendly bases elsewhere, refuel and then return by an indirect route. This novel concept was first introduced on the night of 20/21 June in a mission against the Zeppelin plant at Friedrichshafen. This factory, located close to Lake Constance (*Bodensee*) in southern Germany and close to neutral Switzerland, was identified in June 1943, as being engaged in the manufacturing of the very efficient '*Würzburg*' radar sets which were so vital to its defence. The first such radars were introduced to control the numerous heavy flak batteries while the introduction of the '*Giant Würzburg*' set saw a new standard in accuracy. With this formidable 'instrument of darkness', the

Ground-Control Interception (GCI) teams could obtain readings accurate to within $1/10^{th}$ of a degree at a range of 25 miles (40 km) and locate a Lancaster's height to within a few hundred feet. For Bomber Command this was an opportunity to set back the enemy's efforts to locate and destroy bombers. As an added incentive, the plant was also thought by some to be involved in the manufacture of the propellant tanks and body sections for long-range rocket (V) weapons.

Operation *Bellicose* was therefore hastily planned to take place at the first opportunity during the next period of a full moon. The task was entrusted to No. 5 Group. Such a mission required a great deal of good fortune if heavy losses were not to result and it was carefully planned. The Pathfinder (PFF) aircraft used the 'offset' marking system, dropping their flares some distance from the actual aiming

Continued on page 64

Left, above and right: This standard Lancaster B.I, R5689, VN-N, of No. 50 Squadron, became famous the world over when it was taken up for the benefit of press photographers in August 1942. A month later, on 18/19 September, she crash-landed at Thurlby when returning from a minelaying sortie and burnt out. She had flown 138 hours in total.

also stronger than forecast, all of which made for difficult aiming. After the initial bombing had been directed at the flare-marked position, a second wave of aircraft carried out their timed runs. No Lancasters from the sixty-strong force were lost, although eight required repairs in North Africa after a ten-hour duration mission time. Subsequent photo-analysis revealed that the factory complex had been hit by at least 10 per cent of the bombs released.

On the night of 31 July/1 August from a force of 630 heavy bombers, no fewer than 113 were Lancasters. Against this impressive build-up of strength, losses remained tiny – just two or three Lancasters being lost per mission most nights, with occasional blips such as over Frankfurt on the night of 24/25 August when six failed to return, or over Essen on the night of 16/17 September when nine were lost.

Attempts at 'precision' attacks continued to be made. One such was Operation *Robinson,* an attempt to destroy the massive Schneider iron and steel works, France's main armament plant at Le Creusot, France, which was at that time busy turning out heavy artillery guns for the German Army. Compared to targets in Germany this was an 'easy' run with regard to distance, but was complicated by the fact that it was deemed essential to minimise French casualties and so a normal

Far left: A 50 Squadron Lancaster comes into land, probably at Skellingthorpe. The wartime censor has erased the 'Monica' aerial from under the rear turret. The Lancasters of 50 Squadron would fly more operations than any other in 5 Group.

point to guide the bombers in without the resulting smoke obscuring the actual target zone itself. The bombers were also trained to employ the 'time-and-distance' from a bombing run to take advantage of this. To further confuse the enemy, an alternate target was to be simultaneously attacked, in this case the Italian Naval base of La Spezia, Liguria, in northern Italy. The Lancasters were then to fly on to the North African air bases of Bilda and Maison Blanc in newly-liberated French Algeria for refuelling and/or repairs.

In essence, the raid, which took place on 20/21 June, was led by the deputy commander designate, Wing Commander Cosme Lockwood Gomm of No. 467 Squadron, with four Lancasters from No. 97 Squadron as Pathfinders. The bright moonlight and the strong flak defences, (approximately sixteen heavy and sixteen light flak guns and twenty-five searchlights), forced the attacks to be made at 5,000 ft (1,524 m) higher altitudes than originally planned. The wind was

War at the sharp end: a graphic close-up view of the bullet-riddled rear turret of ED413 'M' seen after its return from a raid on Oberhausen on 15 June 1943. The occupant, Sgt P F Hayes of 57 Squadron, was killed. This machine was one of a force of 197 Lancasters taking part in the raid. Two hundred and sixty-seven buildings were destroyed and 584 seriously damaged, with 85 killed and 258 injured, according to German reports.

W4154 was a veteran Lancaster that flew on many of the very early raids to France. She is photographed here late in her career with 1662 HCU (Heavy Conversion Unit). The Rose turret was a late-war modification featuring a turret fitted with twin 0.50 inch Browning machine guns, devised as a result of co-operation between Air Vice-Marshal Edward Rice, commander of 1 Group, and Alfred Rose of the engineering firm of Rose Brothers.

to show, many of the bombs had fallen well short and some had impacted on the very French workers' houses they had attempted to avoid. Nor was the plant put out of commission, and those parts that were hit were back in full production within a few months.

It was back to area bombing then, as much as the increasingly bad weather conditions over the Reich allowed – as shown when both an attack on Duisburg on the night of 6/7 September and against Frankfurt the following night, were largely abortive. The PFF tactics were continually modified in the light of experience and the introduction of new equipment. These aircraft were often divided into two groups: one as 'Illuminators' dropping flares and then Visual Markers to indicate the aiming point; and the second, the 'Backers-Up' dropping incendiaries on top of these markers to provide further definition.

These pyrotechnics reached a new level of sophistication on the night of 10/11 September, with the deployment of a specially adapted 4,000 lb (1,814.36 kg) incendiary canister, known from the colour of its overwhelmingly and unmistakably intense flash effect as 'Pink Pansy'. After the Pathfinders had dropped red flares to mark the city's western boundary and green flares to mark the eastern, like the starboard and port lights of a liner, this awesome illumination was deposited in the middle to indicate the exact aiming point and the bomber stream simply flew between the boundaries and dropped their cargoes. For the loss of five of the participating Lancasters, out of 479 heavy bombers, plus twenty-eight of other types, this proved a costly debut for the method but was deemed successful.

The year's final milestone was an attack on Turin in Italy, mounted on the night of 21/22 December when 119 from a total strength of 137 Bomber Command aircraft were Lancasters, eight being casualties. The year of 1943 promised even greater concentrations and on the night of 16/17 January 190 of the 201 heavy bombers which attacked Berlin were Lancasters. They only lost one of their number, but a repeat strike the following night found the Germans more prepared and nineteen Lancasters were destroyed, the heaviest single night's casualties to date. This had no effect on their continued deployment, however.

The attack on Berlin on the night of 16/17 January was a bold move since much of Bomber Command's strength at the time was engaged in area bombing the French naval ports of L'Orient, St. Nazaire and La Pallice which were being used as the main bases

night attack was ruled out as lacking the required finesse. A daylight raid was therefore mounted, with nine Lancaster Squadrons from No. 5 Group, led by Wing Commander Leonard Slee of No. 49 Squadron. All the contributing units, which totalled 94 Lancasters, undertook several days of intensive mission training on low-level tactics. No. 617 Squadron also contributed six Lancasters in a subsidiary raid on the Henri Paul power station complex located at Montchanin.

The mission itself was undertaken on 17 October and achieved complete surprise. No German fighters intercepted the bombers on their way in to the target in the late afternoon and attacks were made from 7,500 ft (2,286 m) altitudes, largely inconvenienced by the defending flak batteries. All types of ordnance were unloaded over the target from 4,000 lb 'Cookies' – high capacity, impact-fused bombs – down to incendiaries, and the force returned home with the loss of just one aircraft. There was great jubilation and a great success was announced, Harris claiming that it was a "brilliantly executed and highly successful operation" and that in less than five minutes, the force had, "deprived the enemy of one of his major sources of armament supply." In truth, as subsequent photo reconnaissance was

Continued on page 70

Far left: An example of Lancaster 'nose art' depicting an attractive 'Lonesome Lola', with an impressive tally of operations. This was a No.9 Squadron machine, LL845, WS-L, which went on to complete 97 missions before being retired in August 1945 and scrapped in January 1947.

Left: A less than glamorous female, 'Cutty Sark II' appeared on the nose of LL853, WS-W also of No.9 Squadron. The same artist – apparently enthused by brands of Scotch whisky – also decorated the well-known W4964, WS-J, 'Johnny Walker'.

49 Squadron Lancasters in the light evening mist form a peaceful scene as they await the next night's mission. Based at Scampton the unit received its Lancasters in 1942 and from there moved successively to Dunholme Lodge, Fiskerton and Fulbeck by 1944. In April 1945 the unit moved to Syerston, its last wartime move.

Right: Lancaster mid-upper gunners often joked that they were the most vulnerable crew member since they sat above 'bullseye' roundels. There was also the constant danger from Flak: here a crew member holds a twelve-inch ruler against a gaping Flak hole at almost 'bullseye' position.

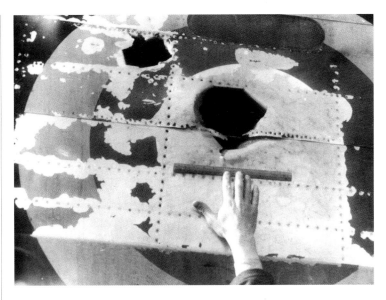

Far right: The Lancaster was tough! PD217 EM-Z of 207 Squadron returned from Stuttgart with considerably less wing than with which she set out, following a mid-air collision with another Lancaster from 57 Squadron in the bomber stream while over the city on 13 September 1944. Of 204 Lancasters despatched that night, four failed to return.

One of the many dangers faced by Lancaster crews was that of falling bombs from above. In the photograph (right), the rear gunner would have suffered a terrifying experience as a 500 lb bomb missed his turret by inches. Sadly, the photograph far right shows that the rear gunner of this aircraft was not so lucky, his turret being sheared off completely.

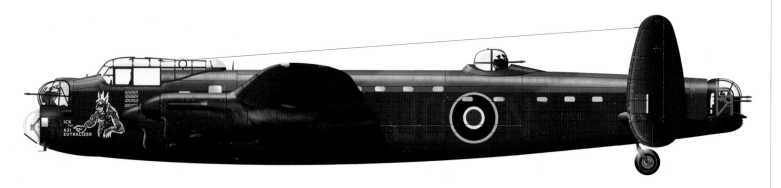

'Nick The Nazi Neutralizer'
Avro Lancaster B.I LM130 JO-N
of No. 463 Squadron RAAF,
Waddington 1944. Pilot Flg. Off.
Hatram. This aircraft came on
strength in May 1944 and
crashed at Metheringham
11 March 1945.

With engines thundering, a
Lancaster prepares to go to war
under the cover of darkness.

Flt. Lt. Playford of Toronto shakes hands with Sgt. W. Hearn of Kent, the NCO in charge of ground crew. The other ground crew are, from left to right: LAC. J. Cowls, Cpl. R. Withey, LAC. J. Robinson and AC. J. Hale. The Lancaster is ND458, HW-A, 'Able Mabel', a 121-mission veteran of 100 Squadron.

for the German U-boat fleet which was decimating Allied convoys in the Atlantic. Despite this, Harris directed 201 heavy bombers, 190 of them Lancasters, against the German capital. The city had not been visited for more than a year and it was hoped the new tactics would improve results. The hope proved illusory for again bad weather nullified the improved target marking and accuracy was poor. The weather improved the following night and 187 bombers, including 170 Lancasters, repeated the attack, but, again, results were spasmodic and nineteen Lancasters failed to return, an eleven per cent casualty rate. Berlin was therefore again reluctantly abandoned for a while as being too ambitious a target as yet.

By February 1943, almost a year after her first war mission, another important milestone in the Lancaster story was reached; the swelling production lines had made the Avro Lancaster the most numerous aircraft type in Bomber Command. By the late summer no fewer than eighteen squadrons were Lancaster-equipped. The Pathfinders were later aided by the development of the well known 'Oboe' navigation system, which enabled single Lancasters equipped with the necessary receiver/transponders to use signals from UK-based radar stations to determine range and the bearing on the range for more precise location. 'Oboe' was initially used on 5 March 1943, when the Krupp works at Essen were the first target of what was known as the Battle of the Ruhr. Five further attacks were made on this target, culminating with that of 25 July, these being interspaced with raids on Duisburg and the 4/5 May attack on Dortmund, which saw no fewer than 255 Lancasters deployed for a loss of six. This was repeated on the night of 23/24 May when Lancasters contributed

343 machines to a force of 826 bombers for the loss of eight. The 'Gee-H' system – adopted to the twin-range of 'H' principle – was then subsequently developed from 'Oboe' to enable wider usage. Here, the position of the aircraft was determined by measuring its range from two ground beacons. The accuracy of measurement of range depended on the accuracy of the pulse alignment.

Yet another attempt to damage Berlin was made on the night of 1/2 March, Lancasters contributing 156 machines, more than half

Wing Commander Guy Penrose Gibson VC, DSO & Bar, DFC, poses in a sea of poppies at Scampton above left, and above, in a more formal pose. The success of the Dambusters eclipsed Gibson's previous outstanding record and gave him a place in history. He was awarded the Victoria Cross for the highest gallantry in the face of the enemy that could be awarded to any member of the British and Commonwealth forces. He became the most highly decorated pilot in the RAF and a national hero.

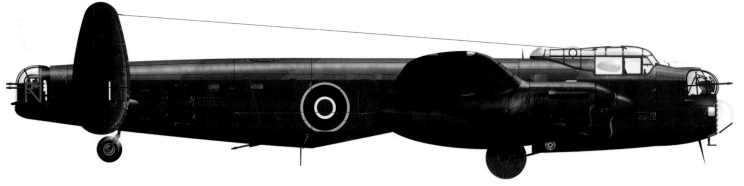

Guy Gibson's Lancaster AJ-G, ED932 as used on the Dams Raid on 16/17 May 1943.

A Type 464 Lancaster drops a full sized 'Upkeep' bouncing during trials in May 1943.

the 302-strong force. Hopes were high but were again to be dashed; the sheer size of the city resulted in an overwhelming and confusing plethora of signals being received from the H2S. A re-think was clearly required. At home the AOC Bomber Command initiated a 'new broom' policy and replaced several of his subordinates, with Air Vice Marshal the Hon. Ralph Cochrane being appointed in command of No. 5 Group, and Air Marshal Sir Robert Saundby emplaced as Harris' deputy. Saundby was as fixated on area bombing as Harris which thus ensured a rigid harmony of thinking at the top of the Command. If Berlin was beyond them yet, the industrial heartland of the Ruhr Valley was not.

The most famous Lancaster mission of all was carried out on the night of 16/17 May, and, although itself atypical of their wartime missions, received enormous publicity at the time and has been immortalised since in film and books to become a legend. No. 617 Squadron, newly put together with selected aircrew as an elite unit, and armed with a series of unique weapons designed by Barnes Wallis, carried out the first of a whole series of attacks against major dams in the Ruhr. The aim was to cut the supply of hydroelectricity feeding the German war machine 'at a stroke'. The novelty of it all, the precision of the attacks, the dramatic impact it made and the lurid headlines it generated, all tended to conceal the fact that the results,

with regard to the effect on the German economy, were less than hoped for. No matter; 'The Dambusters', as they became, were accorded the status of national icons and were an enormous fillip to the nation's jaded morale at this stage of the war. It showed that Britain could still innovate and deliver and the Lancaster became as famous in its way as the Supermarine Spitfire had almost three years earlier.

For these dam-busting missions the special 'Upkeep' 'bouncing bomb' was utilised. The Ruhr Dams (the Möhne, Sorpe, Eder, Lister, Ennepe, Diemel and Henne) had long been on the list of desirable targets for Bomber Command to strike at, but they had always lacked a suitable weapon. The Lancaster had been designed to carry aerial torpedoes, but despite this they were not used as the dams were protected by anti-torpedo nets. Tests at the Nant-y-Gro Dam near the Rhayader reservoirs in mid-Wales had indicated that if the torpedoes could be detonated in contact with the base of the dam then under 3 tons of explosives would suffice to burst them, whereas they were virtually immune from normal bombing.

Wallis came up with a revolutionary concept in which a spherical mine could be released in such a way that a backspin was induced so that it would literally bounce like a skipping stone across the water surface, over the netting and into the face of the dam. Once halted this mine would sink down, still rotating but adjacent to the dam. At the base of the target, at some 30 ft (9 m) down, the hydrostatic pressure on a trio of pistols would be automatically triggered as the pressure equalised, and the dam breached. The final product was a 9,250 lb (4,196 kg) cylindrically-shaped casing, 5 ft (1.5 m) in length and with a diameter of 4ft 2in (1.2 m) containing 6000 lb (2,721 kg) of explosives, which were considered sufficient for the required job.

In order to accommodate this weapon a force of twenty-three specially modified Lancasters, termed by Avro's drawing Z2852 at the time as the 'Type 464 Provisioning', (later as the BIII [Special]) was created. The changes included taking out the bomb bay doors and in their place Vickers-built v-formed strut arms designed to hold the canister-like bombs were fixed. The mid-upper gun turret was taken out and its pump was instead used to drive a hydraulic motor, which imparted the required spin of 500 rpm via a belt drive to the weapon. The displaced gunner was kept aboard and manned the front turret while its normal occupant, the front gunner/bomb-aimer was able to concentrate on his task.

Both pages: A Lancaster B.III, ED817, AJ-C of No. 617 Squadron, was one of three prototypes designed to carry the dam-busting weapon (code name 'Upkeep') designed by Dr. Barnes Wallis. Twenty-three aircraft were converted and although this particular machine did not take part in the raid another 'C-Charlie' did. Principal identifying features were the absence of the mid-upper turret and the cut-away bomb bay.

Although of poor quality, this view of Guy Gibson's Type 464 Lancaster shows the forward spotlight fitted in the nose camera aperture and the extra VHF aerial which enabled the aircraft to communicate with each other on the Dams Raid. The light patches on the leading edge of the wings are cable cutters.

Because the 'Upkeep' had to be released at the specific very low-level height of just 60 ft (18 m) above the water, and at a release speed of between 240 to 250 mph (386 to 402 km/h) in order for it to work, a clever device was installed with angled lamps positioned in the nose and the bomb bay, whose illuminated cones merged on the water's surface only at the exact required altitude. Several secret tests of this mine were conducted at Chesil Beach, Dorset and Reculver, Kent in 1942-43. Once the actual German dams had been filled by the winter rains, preparations for the attacks went ahead on 16 May, to take advantage of a full moon.

Led by Wing Commander Guy Gibson, nineteen of the Lancasters took off from RAF Scampton in three groups, their targets being the Möhne, Eder and Sorpe Dams. One Lancaster aborted, five Lancasters were destroyed before they even reached the Ruhr, and another turned back with severe flak damage; a seventh flew so low over the sea that it lost its mine and also had to turn back, while an eighth failed to find any target and took its mine home again. The remaining Lancasters pressed on to the target and these made their attacks against four of the dams.

Gibson himself dropped the first mine at 0028, after first making a trial run without a release, but the explosion occurred some distance from the dam. Next in was Flight Lieutenant J.V. Hopgood, but the fully-alert German anti-aircraft gunners hit his Lancaster, which, fatally damaged, released late before blowing up. The mine bounced right over the dam itself, striking the power station below. The third attack was made by Flight Lieutenant H.B.M. Martin, and this too failed to act as hoped, the mine again exploding away from the dam, but it may have added something to the cumulative effect on the foundations. However, it was the fourth Lancaster, piloted by Squadron Leader H.M.Young, which made the perfect attack, its mine bouncing three times and sinking down to explode as planned. The dam was already beginning to give way when the fifth bomber with Flight Lieutenant D.J. Maltby at the controls also scored a direct hit. Between them, the two accurate deliveries opened up a 250 ft (76.2 m) wide breach in the dam. Unfortunately, a second Lancaster paid the price when Young's machine was shot down over the North Sea on the return leg.

Three Lancasters of this group still retained their mines and Gibson led these to the second target, the Eder Dam. The approach to this target was tricky and required steep turns; multiple attempts

An aerial reconnaissance photograph of the breached Möhne Dam, the morning after the raid.

were made without release before firstly Flight Lieutenant D. J. Shannon and then Squadron Leader H. E. Maudslay made positive attacks. Shannon's mine detonated close to the dam, but not at the centre section while the other also failed, striking the parapet and detonating, but so damaging this aircraft that it fell prey to German defences while crossing the Dutch frontier. In the end it was the last Lancaster of the trio, piloted by Pilot Officer L. G. Knight, who, after one trial attempt, dropped correctly and whose bomb opened up a 100 ft (30.48 m) breach in the dam, which the outpouring rush of the waters rapidly increased.

The Sorpe Dams, being of different construction, were attacked differently, with the Lancasters making their runs along the line of the dam itself in order to drop a non-spinning mine. Visibility was poor and again many attempts had to be made before the actual release attacks took place. Although both attackers, Flight Lieutenant J. C. McCarthy and Flight Sergeant Ken Brown, scored the required direct hits, the dam remained inviolate, although the damage inflicted was sufficient to force the Germans to later lower the water level of the reservoirs.

A further Lancaster piloted by Flight Lieutenant Bill Townsend attacked the Bever Dam, mistaken for the Ennepe Dam, an alternate target, but without success. For the loss of eight Lancasters two of the principal dams had been taken out, with the release of 4,096,500 ft^3 (116,000,000 sq.m) of water from the Möhne reservoir and 5,438,458 ft^3 (154,000,000 sq.m) from the Eder. This outpouring destroyed eleven factories, 25 bridges, damaged many more, and inundated coal mines and other infrastructure for a period, while 1,300 civilians were drowned, most of them foreign labourers, and many thousands of animals. However, both dams were quickly repaired and the Germans had both of them back in full service again before the year was out. Nonetheless, it was a brilliant propaganda coup for Harris, and helped offset the disappointing results elsewhere, while lifting morale at home.

The area bombing offensive continued and reached a new level of annihilation with the destruction of the principal German port city of Hamburg in a series of devastating attacks which took place over a ten day period between 24 July and 3 August – the aptly-named Operation *Gomorrah*. Here the German radar defence was first bamboozled by the use of 'Window'. In the initial attack 791 heavy bombers contributed, of which 354 were Lancasters drawn

The Möhne Dam pictured on the morning after the raid, with the waters still gushing out of the breach. In the foreground are the anti-torpedo nets, which should have protected the structure, after they had been carried away by the outgoing waters.

After the attack on the dams on 16/17 May 1943 the King visited No. 617 Squadron at Scampton to congratulate the crews. He is seen here talking to Flight Lieutenant Harold 'Micky' Martin (later Air Marshal Sir Harold), while Wing Commander Guy Gibson is nearest the camera.

Right: On the way to the Sorpe Dam, Flight Lieutenant R. Barlow's aircraft was believed hit by Flak and then flew into high-tension cables. The aircraft crashed near the border between Holland and Germany, leaving no survivors. After hitting the ground the Lancaster broke up, and the 'Upkeep' weapon was torn loose and ended up in a small wood. Here Nazi Party members look on as a Luftwaffe pilot, wearing the Knights Cross, discusses the unexploded weapon the next day. The weapon itself presented few surprises, as the Luftwaffe had experimented with a similar device for use against warships.

from nineteen different squadrons and, of these, 728 delivered their bomb cargoes in less than one hour. Bombing was loose with a 'creep back' of six miles (9.6 km) from the target zone, which killed 1,500 civilians and caused extensive damage across the central and north-west sectors of the city. A mere twelve bombers were lost in return.

The RAF returned in force on the night of 27/28, with 787 heavy bombers again being led in by H2S-equipped Pathfinder units. This delivery of some 600 bombs, 2,326 tons (2,363,325.10 kg) of high explosives, was much more concentrated on the old town, principally an area two miles (3.2 km) wide by one mile (1.6 km) deep, east of the city centre, which housed workers' houses. The particularly dry and warm weather conditions combined with the tinderbox qualities of the old buildings and the inability of the firefighting teams to reach the seat of the blazes, combined to form the first of a devastating new phenomenon, the *Feuersturm* (Fire Storm). Here the many blazing areas gradually merged, creating their own atmosphere and sucking in winds that reached 150 mph (240 km/h). In the heart of this huge blast furnace temperatures reached an estimated 800 degrees Centigrade (1,500 degrees Fahrenheit). This massive three-hour conflagration incinerated everything in an eight square mile (21 sq.km) area – buildings, vehicles, people, in one all-consuming furnace. Air raid shelters proved death traps as the sheltering thousands were literally baked alive or asphyxiated *en masse* when all the oxygen was sucked out by the fire. An estimated forty-two thousand people, (21,000 women, 13,000 men and 8,000 children), were incinerated that night, and this caused the mass evacuation of most of the remaining populace. Harris espoused the policy, "If you can't hit the works, hit the workers" and this attack was the ultimate expression of his creed. About 6,200 densely-populated acres (25.09 sq.km) had been extinguished and Hitler's Minister of Production, Albert Speer told his *Führer* that if such attacks continued they might bring about a "rapid end to the war."

On the night of 29/30 July, Bomber Command revisited the city with 777 heavy bombers, in order to eliminate what remained of the workers' dwellings in the northern area which had escaped almost intact. An error led instead to the delivery of the bulk of the ordnance into the residential areas just north of the already levelled area. Again there were numerous fires and much devastation was caused, but casualties were less as the bulk of the populace had already fled. The attacking force lost twenty-eight machines. Yet a fourth blow was planned to finish off Hamburg for good, some 740 heavy bombers being sent out on the night of 2/3 August, but this time the weather became the saviour of the city rather than its tormentor and most of the aircraft failed to reach the target, while another thirty bombers were lost. In total some 2,355 bombers had been despatched in the first three raids, of which just 57 (2.4 per cent) were lost, which was considered easily acceptable.

Another attack carried out by Bomber Command at this time was Operation *Hydra*, on the night of 17/18 August, the target being the top secret German Army Research Centre at Peenemünde, located on the western end of the Baltic island of Usedom. Here, key scientists under Dr. Werner von Braun were developing the long-range rocket weapons that were to result in the V-1 and V-2 programmes which so devastated London the following year. The attack was carried out by a force of 596 'heavies', 324 of these being Lancasters drawn from every one of the twenty-two out of the twenty-three existing squadrons equipped with this aircraft, No.617 being the exception. They attacked at a height lower than normal at 8,000 ft (2,438.4 m) and by moonlight, using the 'Master Bomber' concept for the first time; for most aircrew this was their first attempt or experience at precision bombing. The objective was to kill as many of the scientists as possible by destruction of their living quarters, with material destruction of the Experimental Station itself as a secondary objective.

Aiming markers were not accurately laid and although some 1,800 tons of bombs were put down, the results were very disappointing. Some laboratories and offices were damaged but only Doctor Walter Thiel, the Deputy Director, and Chief Engineer Erich Walther among the scientists were killed; unfortunately the majority of casualties were from the Polish slave workers from Camp Trassenheide, which was heavily hit. In total the RAF lost forty machines (24 of them Lancasters), twenty-nine of them to enemy fighters. Although it was claimed that this raid set back research for several weeks the only real material result was that the V-2 Production Plant, which was almost operational, was relocated to the *Mittelwerk*.

With these spectacular missions under their belt and with Hamburg as their inspiration, Bomber Command now turned to the ultimate test, Harris's implacable desire to destroy the German capital from the air and thus bring the war to an end without the need for any invasion. The Battle of Berlin now began in earnest.

EM-Z, LM326, of 207 Squadron gently banks away in a very peaceful English sky, in the autumn of 1943. A few days after this photograph was taken, she was gone, lost over Hannover taking Flight Sergeant Taylor and his crew with her. 207 Squadron flew 385 raids with the Lancaster, losing 131 machines in the process.

One of the thousands of Lancasters turned out by the Castle Bromwich factory on a test flight over the English countryside.

Right: The 1000th Lancaster built at Trafford Park, seen in a commemorative photograph with the female production line worker after whom it was named – Margaret Barber.

Left: DX-O of 57 Squadron is fitted with the early shallow bomb-aimer's blister. The leading edge is covered with a liberal coating of de-icing paste. Part of No.5 Group, this unit received its Lancasters in late 1942 at Scampton, later moving to East Kirkby in August 1943 and then back to Scampton in late 1945.

Below: A Lancaster is caught dramatically in the beam of a Chance Light as it prepares to take off for an operation.

A 207 Squadron Lancaster seen in flight while on an air test in 1942. The squadron received its Lancasters in January 1942 and commenced operations on them in April 1942. The unit formed part of No.5 Group and operated successively from Waddington, Bottlesford, Swinderby, Langar, Spilsby, Methwold and Tuddenham during the war.

Searchlights illuminate the cloud base as a 103 Squadron Lancaster prepares for take-off. Part of No.1 Group, this squadron replaced its Halifaxes with Lancasters in November 1942 and operated throughout the war from Elsham Wolds.

Sgt. Cook, Sgt. Wildeny, F/S. Tear, F/S. Barnes, F/S. Ireland, F/S. Haslam and Sgt. Clark of 576 Squadron pose with ED888, PM-M(2) after its 140th 'op', a Bomber Command record. She would eventually be scrapped in January 1947. Part of No.1 Group, this unit was formed from 'A' and 'B' Flights from No.103 and No.101 Squadrons in November 1943 at Elsham Wolds. It later moved to Fiskerton in October 1944 using a mixed strength of Lancaster I/IIIs.

Right: A vital element of the Lancaster's contribution to the war lay in the commitment of its groundcrews who serviced the aircraft on remote hardstandings in all weather.

An early production Lancaster takes off. Note the heavy exhaust smoke present at full power which was also responsible for coating the wings with lead deposits on operational aircraft.

Below: In 1943, Bomber Command carried out several 'shuttle raids' where Lancasters were sent to bomb targets deep in occupied Europe and instead of returning to the UK, flew on to North Africa to refuel and rearm. This 49 Squadron Lancaster is photographed at Blida in Algeria while preparing for the long flight home.

Left: Wing Commander Campbell Hopcroft, DFC and his 57 Squadron crew pose with DX-F 'Frederick II' at Scampton.

Right: R5727 was sent to Canada to provide a pattern for local Lancaster production.
The seldom used ventral turret can clearly be seen in this view. The aircraft later received the registration CF-CMS.

Below: The seventeenth Lancaster to be built, L7540, is given a thorough going-over for the benefit of the press. This aircraft served with 44 Squadron and was eventually SOC in April 1944.

Below right: Some Lancasters were fitted with dual controls at HCUs to enable pilots to be trained more easily in the handling of this big aircraft.

A 467 Squadron Lancaster of the RAAF, photographed over the target area. Many squadrons in 5 Group painted the aircraft codes on the tailplanes to help squadrons identify their own aircraft when forming up for daylight ops. Formed at Scampton in November 1942, it later moved to Bottesford operating B.I/IIIs. A move to Waddington took place in November 1943 and then to Metheringham in January 1945.

The Lancaster's 102 ft wingspan is shown to good effect in this air-to-air study of an uncoded machine.

5 A War of Attrition

There was little doubt that the Lancaster was the heavy bomber par excellence as far as the Royal Air Force was concerned. No matter what challenges it placed in her path, she met and overcame them. Now that it had the aircraft and had fitted it with every aid possible, the RAF set about proving its theory that she could win the war single-handed. It was to prove a tough learning curve for all concerned and only an aircraft as resilient as the Lancaster could have survived the trials and tribulations. Finally, with the end of the war in Europe, thoughts turned to the distant Pacific, but it was not to be. Post-war the advent of the Atomic Bomb meant that one aircraft could do the job previously done by a thousand and the Lancaster was suddenly surplus to requirements. Nonetheless she soldiered on in many guises, both at home and abroad, and several worthwhile and long-serving successors sprang from her sound basic design.

57 Squadron Lancasters at dusk, at Scampton or East Kirby, waiting for the call to arms.

BERLIN was a target that was heavily defended by what the Air Ministry subsequently described as the most "formidable and flexible" defences against air attack. First introduced in August 1943, the German night fighter defences had substantially increased in numbers and under the *Wilde Sau* (Wild Sow) system introduced by *Oberst* Hajo Herrmann, single-engined fighters guided by searchlight teams and pyrotechnic signals, reinforced the twin-engined machines, which, in turn expanded from 550 machines to 775, now hunted in groups rather than singly under the *Zahme Sau* (Tame Sow) system and met the bomber streams further out, even while they were still over the North Sea, giving the German fighters a longer timeframe in which to make repeated attacks. Better models (G-1 and G-6) of the formidable Ju 88 appeared and armament improved with the introduction of the powerful 30-mm cannon and an upward-firing 20-mm cannon, which continued to capitalise on the lack of the Lancaster's ventral defence. The German *Kammhuber*[1] Ground Control Interception (GCI) radar chain line of defence, was also deepened with additional stations built further back from the coast and made more effective so that more than one fighter could be controlled at a time.

Coupled with these improvements, the German flak arm also expanded – production of heavy anti-aircraft guns and searchlights vastly expanded, in some cases doubling, which enabled larger concentrations of batteries (*Grossbatterien*) to be located around important targets. Between August 1943 and June 1944 the number of guns in each individual battery increased first to 6/8 guns and then to 8/12 guns per battery. By early 1944 30-40 new heavy gun batteries per month were being emplaced, and the size and power of these guns was also enhanced with *Flakeinsatzführer* personnel introduced to better co-ordinate them.

Despite the growth of more efficient defences, 'Bomber' Harris remained convinced it was a battle that could be won, although at some cost. He declared he would "wreck Berlin from end to end", and although that might cost the Allies between 400-500 aircraft, "It will cost Germany the war." He set about proving that his command was up to that task. The battle itself can be said to have lasted from 18 November 1943 until 24 March 1944, and Berlin suffered sixteen major air attacks in that period. Losses to Bomber Command were indeed severe, and as other heavies, the Stirling and the Halifax, suffered and had to be withdrawn, the Lancaster was forced more and more to be the mainstay of the campaign.

In total 492 heavy bombers were lost during the Berlin battle. Nor was this all since the RAF heavy bombers had by no means been confined exclusively to attacking the German capital and, during the same period of time, a further 550 were destroyed over other parts of the Reich. The worst disaster came about on the night of 30/31 March during the disastrous Nuremberg mission. Some 782 heavy bombers were despatched against this city, of which 57 aborted the mission. Of those 725 bombers that pressed on, 96 were destroyed, 64 of them being Lancasters. Thirty-two Halifaxes and six additional bombers were so damaged on reaching home that they were write-offs. Casualties included 545 dead, 150 Officers, 24 Warrant Officers and 371 NCOs, with 159 others becoming POWs. Little wonder that this night went down in Bomber Command history as 'Black Friday'.

This raid was mounted despite a reconnaissance report from a De Havilland Mosquito the previous afternoon that there was little

---

[1.] So-named after Colonel Josef Kammhuber, first commander of the *Luftwaffe's* Night Fighter force.

This early production Lancaster, L7540, OL-U, fitted with an unfaired mid-upper turret, operated with No. 83 Squadron. She had previously flown with No. 44 (Rhodesia) Squadron whose KM unit code can still be seen under the OL code. No. 88 Squadron was part of Nos.5 and 8 Groups and was formed on Lancasters in the Spring of 1942. It operated from Scampton, Wyton and was at Coningsby by April 1944. L7540 was eventually SOC (struck off charge) in April 1944.

chance of cloud cover protecting the stream from the bright moonlight along the 265 miles (426.47 km) across Germany *en route* to the target, but that Nuremberg itself was cloudy. A supplementary report advised that there were large strato-cumulus with tops to about 8,000 ft (2,438 m) over the target, with patchy cloud between 15,000 ft (4,572 m) and 16,000 ft (4,876 m), which would make target marking difficult. Despite this forecast the raid still went ahead as planned and, worse, the participating squadrons, both Pathfinder

and Bomber Command, were not advised of these conditions. Nor did airborne reports about a radical change in the wind direction to due west get through. Diversionary feints did not fool Major General Josef Schmid, commander of the Luftwaffe's XII Air Corps, or his combat-seasoned pilots, or those manning the underground Deelen operations centre, and soon some 246 night fighters began to assemble over the 'Ida' and 'Otto' radar beacons. The first bomber was shot down just after midnight, and a dozen more followed before the stream had crossed the Rhine. The main bulk of the heavy bombers were now heading directly for the defending fighters in clear visibility. Moreover, the big bombers began emitting long, white vapour trails at altitudes of 19,000 ft (5,791 m) to 20,000 ft (6,096 m), which further aided the Germans to home in.

The standard German night fighter tactic had been to approach about 1,500 ft (457.2 m) below the Lancaster, sharply raise the nose of their fighters and as the target crossed the gunsight, fire with everything they had. This certainly did the job but was risky. With the new tactics they merely had to approach the target from below and astern and their powerful fixed armament had no problems dealing with any heavy bomber.

With the unprotected underbellies of the Lancasters providing wide targets and an undetectable ventral approach to their Ikaria upward-firing 20-mm *MG FF/M* cannon, which fired a 90 g, thin-walled, high-explosive *Minengeschoss* (mine shell) at 523 rpm, the *Luftwaffe's* night fighter pilots had a field day. *Oberleutnant* Helmut Schulte alone destroyed four of the four-engined bombers very economically, firing just fifty-six cannon shells; a second German pilot, *Leutnant* Wilhelm Seuss, matched that score, and survived the explosion as one of his victims blew up in mid-air above him as the bomb cargo detonated. Even these scores were bettered by *Oberleutnant* Martin Becker, who personally took out six bombers – three Lancasters and three Halifaxes – in thirty minutes and later added a seventh to his night's tally. During the 220 mile (354 km) 'Long Leg' from Liege to the southern turn toward the target zone, 59 bombers had been shot down, 41 of them Lancasters.

Seventy-five miles were left to cover and, under continued assault and encountering thick cloud and increasing side winds, many of the force were misled by their radar and by the fact that some of the marking flares had been dropped in the wrong places, up to thirty miles (48 km) north to sixty miles (96.5 km) south of Nuremberg. Despite the odds, many did manage to bomb the target, killing 133 civilians and injuring 412 others, and destroying or damaging 96 factories and over four thousand houses. The Germans described the damage as 'medium/small'. On the Nuremberg raid, just about everything that could go wrong with a heavy bomber mission had done so. Head winds faced the bombers for the return flight and their scattered aircraft continued to take casualties, including one mid-air collision. The Germans lost ten fighters. Many years later 'Butch' Harris blamed the weather and the lack of heavy defensive firepower.

In an effort to disrupt the German night fighters R/T controls, which operated in the 30-33, 38.3-42.5 and 48-52 MHz frequency bands, the RAF introduced the ABC system to the Lancaster in October 1943. This apparatus, developed by the Telecommunications Research Establishment (TRE) was the ARI 5558. It consisted of a panoramic receiver and aerial and three transmitters, each with their own aerial. There was also a visual indicator, which was scanned by a Special Operator, an additional crew member who was fluent in the German language. On missions such aircraft flew with the bomber stream and listened out for and then jammed the German transmissions. No. 101 Squadron trialled this device in combat on the night of 7/8 October and it was christened the 'Airborne Cigar'.

What has since been claimed as the longest combat flight by a Lancaster, took place on 24 April 1944, by No. 630 Squadron, based at East Kirby, Lincolnshire. They attacked Munich via a circuitous approach route which involved crossing the French Alps across the north of Italy and thence to the target, returning to an airfield in southern England due to the tightness of the fuel situation. The whole outward and homeward route totalled over 2,000 miles (3,219 km). One aircraft, 'K' for Kitty, with a mixed Australian, British and New Zealand crew typical of the period, and piloted by New Zealander Joe Lennon, opted arbitrarily to land back at its home base instead, and this was achieved after a total flying time of ten hours, twenty-five minutes. According to the flight engineer, Harry Parkins, the engines cut out as they began to taxi back to the dispersal area. They received a reprimand by the Flight Commander for risking the aircraft and their lives, and congratulations from the Group Captain for getting away with it![2]

Meanwhile, the disaster of Nuremberg had been followed by an urgent re-evaluation of Lancaster tactics. Despatching every single available aircraft against a single target was clearly not a policy to be followed until such time as the German defences had been beaten down further. Instead, the decision was made to split the attacks between two or more targets on the same night whenever possible. There were exceptions to this ruling of course, but to aid the

[2] See: *WW2 People's War: An Archive of World War Two Memories*, ID A8955624, 29 January 2006.

This Lancaster B I Special, PD119, YZ-J, entered service with 617 Squadron in March 1945. As it was mainly intended to operate during daylight, it was camouflaged in the day-bomber scheme with pale blue undersurfaces. Note the lack of nose and mid-upper turrets.

Another view of the Lancaster B.I Special, PD119, YZ-J. Note the the black port fin probably indicating it had been taken from a conventionally camouflaged Lancaster. The aircraft went on to serve in 156 and 15 Squadrons and finally went to the RAE, Shoeburyness by May 1951.

Pathfinders, whose own tasks were thus made more difficult, two Lancaster squadrons, Nos. 83 and 97, thus had Very High Frequency (VHF) radio equipment fitted and were operationally handed over to No. 5 Group. This specialist group, under the direction of its commander, Air Marshal Ralph Cochrane, had been working semi-independently and developing its own 'Master Bomber' techniques in attacks on such important targets as Toulouse aircraft factory on 5/6 April and against Brunswick on 22/23 of the same month.

This was part and parcel of the new brief, in part an unspoken admission that area bombing had so far failed to break the will of the German populace and, with the impending landings of the British, Canadian and American armies at Normandy in France scheduled for June, the softening-up of the enemy's lines of communications and,

nearer the time, fortifications, became part of Bomber Command's brief, however reluctantly. Harris hated this 'diversion' of his strength to aid the armies as much as he had done anti-submarine operations to aid the Navy, but the Chiefs of Staff insisted. Once the troops were ashore, isolating the enemy from reinforcements became a priority; indeed the first 'Tallboys' were dropped on the Saumur rail tunnel on the night of 8/9 June. Not that area bombing of cities was abandoned of course, but other important precision attacks included the tactical saturation bombing of German army concentrations in northern France.

In November 1944, Nos. 9 and 617 Squadrons employed the newly-developed 'Tallboy' bomb to finish off the German battleship *Tirpitz* in her Norwegian lair. By this date, in all truth, her fighting

A Lancaster B.III, LM418, PG-S in service with No. 619 Squadron then based at Coningsby and photographed in February 1944. This aircraft was eventually destroyed in a crash-landing and fire at Woodbridge on 30/31 March 1944, after returning from a sortie against the city of Nuremberg with two engines out of action. Part of No.5 Group, the squadron formed at Woodhall Spa in April 1943 from ex No. 617 Lancasters. The squadron then operated successively from Coningsby, Dunholme Lodge, Strubby and finally Skellingthorpe, where it disbanded in September 1945.

A bombing photograph taken by Flt. Lt. Bob Knight of 617 Squadron, taken on 12 November 1944 showing smoke already over the Battleship Tirpitz after at least one direct hit. The explosion of a third 'Tallboy' which overshot the target and landed just on the edge of the island, can also clearly be seen.

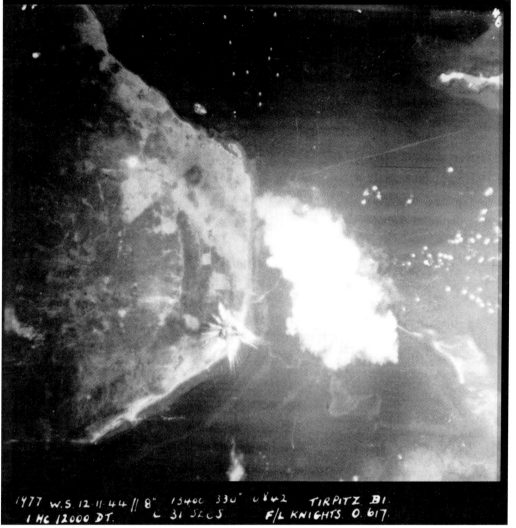

the Lancasters would have a reasonable chance of hitting her. Her defences, apart from her own guns, included smokescreens and nearby fighter bases, but it was considered that stripped-down Lancasters could both reach her, and, given some luck, surprise the defences.

Two earlier attempts had already been made using 'Tallboy' bombs and Johnny Walker 500 lb 'walking' mines, the first while the battleship had been previously based at Kaa Fjord, with the Lancasters flying from the far northern Soviet air base of Yagodnik, close to Archangel. Six Lancasters had crash-landed but the remaining twenty-one had attacked on 15 September, but had only scored one possible hit. The new location of the *Tirpitz,* in Håkøybotn Bay, west of Tromsø, meant that she was just about within the extreme range of stripped-down Lancasters flying from the northernmost UK, and forty bombers from both units moved up to Lossiemouth to make the second attempt. The attack took place on 29 October but, again, was a total failure, no bomb falling close enough to do any significant damage to the leviathan.

On 12 November came a third Lancaster effort, again from Lossiemouth. Wing Commander James Brian 'Willie' Tait led eighteen No. 617 Squadron aircraft and thirteen No. 9 Squadron machines in a final attempt – Operation *Catechism.* Again a chance was taken by unloading the Lancasters' mid-upper gun, which was sacrificed for extra fuel capacity. The Lancasters were advantaged in that, although the weather was clear, the enemy were caught flat-footed and none of the defending German fighters was airborne in time to make interceptions (for which their commander was court martialled and initially received a death sentence, later

career was already long over, having been dive-bombed by the Fleet Air Arm, then severely damaged underwater by Royal Navy limpet mines attached from midget submarines (X-craft) and finally anchored as a static battery off Trondheim. Gravel and sand was packed beneath her to keep her upright so she was not even really afloat, and she was certainly no longer seaworthy or able to sortie against Allied convoys. Despite this, and even in this reduced state, she was a trophy to be prized and, as a bonus, she was totally static so commuted), while the smokescreen which was usually laid around the battleship's anchorage to shield her from the bomb-aimers, was late in being deployed. The bombers therefore had a completely free shot at the stationary giant, and this time made the most of their window of opportunity.

They dropped their 'Tallboys' from heights of between 10,000 and 14,000 ft (3,048 and 4,267 m) with considerable skill, three bombs scoring direct hits and many near misses being observed. One of these penetrated one of *Tirpitz's* main magazines which blew up, taking the roof of a gun turret off, while collateral damage from the near-misses gouged out her under-hull support so that she listed over and finally turned turtle, trapping almost one thousand of her 1,700-man crew. Her upturned hull was gradually scrapped post-war.

The varying and expanding role of the Lancaster as its mission specification reflected the changing priorities of the war and the orders of the Chiefs of Staff are reflected in the way the bomb loads varied. Thanks to that original, (and never utilised) specification to carry the 21-inch (53.34 cm) torpedo, which was a totally unrealistic mission for such an aircraft, that capacious 33 ft (10 m) by 5 ft (1.52 m) bomb bay was able to cope with a huge variety of ordnance.

Early operations in 1942, involving the Lancaster in a maritime, anti-submarine configuration, were soon phased out, but the dual requirement was a concentration of carrying extra fuel to give maximum patrolling range and duration, which limited the ordnance weight. Attacks were expected to be made either against fully-surfaced or partially-submerged submarine targets which were crash-diving to escape. Lancasters did not usually carry depth charges for attacking submerged targets. Only later in the war did submarines stay on the surface to fight it out, but Lancasters were not involved by then. Submarine hulls were tough and any patrolling aircraft required a mix of weapons for either eventuality. Therefore in the few cases were the Lancaster was involved in this type of operation, six 500 lb (226.74 kg) and three 250 lb (113.39 kg) Mk. I, II and II anti-submarine bombs, all fused for semi-submerged attacks were carried, along with five 250 lb (113.39 kg) Semi-Armour Piercing (SAP), tail-armed with instantaneous to 2-second delay fusing for attacking fully surfaced targets.

Other purely maritime-related missions concerned the blockade of the enemy-controlled dockyards, shipbuilding yards and supply ports – not direct action, but sewing the sea lanes and dredged

The Tirpitz did not actually sink, since the water in which it lay was not deep enough. The battleship simply capsized. This photograph was taken some time after the Lancaster raid, as there was very little snow on the ground on the day of the attack. Her rust red-coloured hull was visible from some distance, and many of the Lancaster crews remember seeing the hull appear through the smoke, confirming that their mission was at last complete.

channels to render them unserviceable was the aim, either as part of a more general plan or to bar a specific naval unit or flotilla or convoys from operating. Code-worded 'Gardening', a maximum load of six 1,850 lb (839.14 kg) parachute mines could be embarked, each have a magnetic or an acoustic actuator fitted.

More usual was the direct action approach, which required the elimination of, or at least severe damage to, specific warships, coastal or harbour fortifications and the dockyard facilities themselves. The bomb load more generally employed for this type of mission had the code-word 'Piece' and was built up with a maximum of six 2,000 lb (907.18 kg), Armour Piercing (AP) bombs, with 0.05-second delay tail fuses, to which a further three 500 lb (226.74 kg) Medium Case (MC), SAP or General Purpose (GP), or 250 lb (113.39 kg) GP bombs could often be added.

The earlier, and costly, medium-range, low-level attacks had been conducted with a simple bomb load of six 1,000 lb (453.59 kg) MC or GP long-finned bombs, (3.3) which were tail-armed with varying time delays from 11 seconds up to an hour. This could be supplemented when required on short-range missions by a further three 250 lb (113.39 kg) GP bombs.

Area bombing called for the maximum destruction of housing and a deadly mix of weapons, with blast bombs to take the roofs off whole blocks and thousands of incendiaries and explosive incendiaries to ignite all-consuming conflagrations which could not be contained. The densely-built old Medieval city centres of Germany proved terribly vulnerable to such attacks. When they were on a large enough scale, these gigantic infernos created their own lethal weather system, the 'Fire Storm'. There was no escape from this form of attack and civilians who might have been safe from conventional explosives in deep shelters were simply cremated, such was the intensity of the heat generated.

Bomber Command's own executive codeword for a 'general' area bombing target was the far from subtle 'Arson'. This comprised a 14,000 lb (6,350.29 kg) package of fourteen (3.3.2.3.3) Small Bomb Containers (SBC), each of which contained 236 of the 4 lb (1.8 kg) No. 15 incendiaries and a 1-in-10 mix of explosive incendiaries. The most common Lancaster loading was appropriately enough code-named 'Usual'. A single 4,000 lb (1,814.36 kg) Heavy Case (HC), impact-fused bomb was centrally loaded and flanked by a total of twelve SBCs packed with either two dozen 30 lb (13.6 kg) or 236 4 lb (1.8 kg) No.15 or No.15X incendiaries (3.3.1.3.3).

For heavily industrialised city targets, which called for a blast, demolition and fire scenario, the 'Cookie/Plumduff' loading was introduced. A single 4,000 lb impact-fused, HC bomb filled with Amatol, Minol or Tritonal was loaded centrally, supplemented by three 1,000 lb (453.59 kg), Heavy Explosive (HE) short-finned, short-delay, tail-armed bombs and packaged with a maximum of six SBCs with either the 4 lb (1.8 kg) or the 30 lb (13.6 kg) incendiary bomb. Later, a step-up from this was the 'Plumduff-Plus' loading, with a single 8,000 lb (3,628.73 kg) Mk I or Mk III, HC bomb, (in fact a pair of 4,000 lb (1,814.36 kg) 'Cookies' enclosed in a single

container) which contained 5,361 lb (2,431.70 kg) of Amatex with either barometric or impact fuses, backed up by up to six 500 lb (226.79 kg) MC or GP bombs fitted with a mix of instantaneous or long-delay fuses.

On the occasions when the target was away from the city centres, and concentrated on specifics, such as dockyards, industrial complexes, warehouses, plant and railway marshalling yards, another mix was carried. It was not a common loading, as its codeword 'Abnormal' implied. This was a load that relied on sheer blasting power to do its job and consisted simply of fourteen 1,000 lb (453.59 kg) MC, GP RDX (Cyclotrimethylenetrinitramine) or US short-finned, HE bombs. Fusing was also a mix of instantaneous, nose-armed or long-delay (maximum of 144 hours possible) bombs tail-armed. Thus the instant demolition effect would be compounded by the uncertainty of the delayed-action weapons, which hampered efforts to clear debris and get the site working again.

Specialist Lancaster squadrons were able to deliver precise bomb loads on to more specific targets, with some degree of accuracy; although as the size and pulverising power of these bombs increased less precision was required. The urgency of countering the German V-1 'Doodlebug' launching sites along the European periphery became a priority in 1944, and the RAF developed the 'No-Ball' load for the carpet-bombing blanketing of such sites. The same mix was considered suitable for blotting out radar sites and, after the Allied armies landed in northern France, as a tactical weapon against concentrations of, for example, enemy armour. This load was built around a single 4,000 lb (1,814.36 kg) 'Cookie', with up to eighteen 500 lb (226.79 kg) MC or GP short-finned bombs, with a mixture of instantaneous and delayed action fuses.

We have already mentioned the 12,000 lb (5,443.10 kg), deep penetration, spin-stabilised 'Tallboy', which contained 5,760 lb (2,612.69 kg) of Torpex D and was trip-fused with a 0.01-second delay, which was used against the heavily armoured battleship *Tirpitz* and to penetrate the thick concrete roofs of the German U-boat pens. Special bulged bomb bay doors had to be fitted on the aircraft expected to carry this weapon. In total the Lancaster dropped some 721 'Tallboys' during the war. However, this seemed very little in the scale of things when the 22,000 lb (9,979.03 kg) 'Grand Slam' appeared. As well as U-boat bunkers, many vital German industries had been moved by Albert Speer deep underground and required

A 22,000 lb 'Grand Slam' is seen being released over the Arnsberg Viaduct on 19 March 1945 from a 617 Squadron Lancaster. The 'Grand Slam' was the largest bomb ever carried by an aircraft during the war and in total there were thirty-three B.1 (Special) Lancasters converted to take the bomb. They ranged in serial batches from PB592, PB995-998 and PD112-139. These aircraft were eventually made obsolete in late 1948 and SOC.

similar penetrating power to suffer from harm. The 'Grand Slam' was also spin-stabilised and contained 11,000 lbs (4,989.51 kg) of Torpex D, and even the Lancaster's commodious bomb bay baulked at this weapon. Only the specially-adapted Lancaster-I could carry this monster, and then only with the bomb doors removed altogether and the mid-upper turret, among other fitments, discarded to compensate for the weight. The bomb itself was first successfully tested at the Ashley Walk, Hampshire bombing range on 13 March 1945.

The devastation caused by the 'Grand Slam', what Barnes Wallis described as 'the earthquake effect', was awesome. The Lancaster utilised this weapon for the first time on 14 March 1945, the target being the Bielefeld Viaduct, a stoutly-built construction that had hitherto defied many and all attempts to damage it significantly. In all, some 3,500 tons of bombs had been aimed at this viaduct so far and had failed to harm it. Once again it was No. 617 Squadron which was

entrusted with the delivery and a pair of converted Lancasters piloted by Group Captain J. E. 'Johnny' Fauquier and Squadron Leader Charles 'Jock' Calder loaded up with the 'Grand Slam'. They took off from Woodhall Spa, Lincolnshire on 13 March, and needed the full length of the runway to become airborne, but unfortunately this mission was 'weathered out' due to thick cloud. The next day only Calder's Lancaster was operational and he took off alone to carry out the task. The bomb was dropped from a height of 11,965 ft (3,647 m) at 1648 hrs. The 'Grand Slam' was not a particularly accurate weapon, but it did not have to be. The impact was some 30 yds (27.5 m) from the viaduct but the predicted subterranean pressure wave effect was still powerful enough to demolish two of the arches, which collapsed into the resulting comouflet. Both the eastern and western spans were brought down over lengths of 260 ft (79 m) and 200 ft (61 m) respectively.

JB675 was converted into a Lancaster Mk.VI with Merlin 85 engines and saw service with No. 635 Squadron. Part of No.3 Group, the squadron formed in March 1943 at Graveley from 'C' Flight of No.97 Squadron. They operated a mix of Lancaster B.I/B.IIIs and in 1944 four Mk.VIs were added, of which JB675 above was one. This aircraft was converted by Rolls Royce in November 1943 and was eventually scrapped in 1948.

The Lancaster flew the most symbolic mission of the war against Adolf Hitler's beloved Berghof Alpine retreat on 25 April 1945, and contributed 359 aircraft; their bombs also largely demolished the SS barracks at nearby Berchtesgaden. This seemed a singularly poetic and apt finale to her wartime career but on the same day 359 further Lancasters were also in action hundreds of miles to the north, bombing heavy artillery installations on Wangerooge Island, the easternmost island of the fortified Frisian group off Germany's North Sea coast. Also that same night, yet another Lancaster mission, the very last one of the Second World War, was made when 107 heavy bombers struck the Tonsberg oil refinery, south of Oslo, Norway, which was still producing fuel for Hitler's U-boats. Here too, the very last Lancaster combat loss was taken. No. 463 Squadron had one aircraft from the fourteen committed, that of Flying Officer Arthur

Cox, which was so badly hit that she crashed in nearby neutral Sweden.

With the coming of peace in Europe on 8 May 1945, it was time to take stock. In total some 7,377 Lancasters had taken to the skies, and between March 1942 and May 1945, they equipped no fewer than 56 squadrons in Nos. 1, 3 and 5 Groups, with No. 6 converting from the Halifax, while *all* the Pathfinder squadrons were now flying the Lancaster. They had carried out 156,000 sorties, dropping 608,613 tons of bombs, about twice as much as the Handley-Page Halifax had delivered, and two-thirds of the entire Bomber Command wartime effort. The Lancasters also dropped 51,513,106 incendiaries and laid 12,733 mines. In doing so no fewer than 3,249 Lancasters were lost in action, while a further 487 were destroyed in accidents or badly damaged. This loss rate was reflected in the fact that

A close-up of the Lancaster cockpit framing, showing the pilot's sliding panel and his grab handle for getting in and out of his seat. Note the application of forty mission symbols flown by this aircraft and the single reversed Swastika probably accounts for a Luftwaffe aircraft shot down.

only twenty-four Lancaster bombers managed to fly more than 100 combat missions, and one machine achieved no fewer than 139 operations[3]. Some 228 million gallons (1,037 million litres) of aviation fuel were used.

During the war Allied bombing raids destroyed 3,370,000 German dwellings, killed 593,000 civilians, police, foreigners and displaced persons, including 70,000 children, and injured a further 486,000. Between 1942 and 1944 German aircraft production alone tripled, rising from 15,409 machines, to 24,807 in 1943 and to 40,593

in 1944. From a total of 3,736 Lancasters destroyed, each with a seven-man crew, even if many actually survived, it can be seen that Lancaster aircrew formed a considerable percentage of the 55,000 Bomber Command men who died and the 18,000 who were wounded during the war. To survive a combat tour of thirty missions needed a lot of luck, especially when at some periods there was a 5 per cent casualty rate per mission.

One could say that each man of every crew deserved a medal for braving such odds; what is a fact is that no fewer than eight Lancaster

---

[3.] An ideal candidate for preservation, this aircraft was sold for scrap in 1947.

The Lancaster's main advantage over its rivals was its capacious and uninterrupted bomb-bay. This allowed the 'Lanc' to carry a larger load than any other RAF bomber during the war.

With the coming of peace a less aggressive mission was entrusted to the Lancaster. Operation *Manna* saw the emergency dropping of over 500 tons of essential food supplies by 239 Lancasters from thirty-one Squadrons of both 1 and 3 Groups, to the starving civilians in German-occupied Netherlands, at pre-designated zones at Duindigt, Valkenburg, Waalhaven and Ypenburg airfields, with the full compliance of the enemy. To test the veracity of the Germans an Anglo-Canadian-manned Lancaster, named 'Bad Penny', piloted by Canadian Robert Upcott, made the trial drop on 29 April 1945 successfully. Another humanitarian mission was Operation *Exodus*, the flying home of many thousands of liberated British POWs from prison camps all over Europe, in which task many former Bomber Command Lancasters operated under the aegis of Transport Command. Many Lancasters were stripped out internally to enable each one to accommodate twenty-five persons and the first of three thousand such humanitarian flights took place from Brussels airport, some four days prior to the armistice. About 74,000 POWs were thus repatriated from Germany, with a similar mission, Operation *Dodge*, bringing home British personnel from the Mediterranean Theatre. With that task completed, the Lancaster's job was almost done.

Gradually the big bomber, already a fast fading memory, was rapidly phased out of operational service by the much reduced peacetime RAF. Her place was ultimately to be taken by a handful of the new Avro Lincoln B1 and B2, developments of the Lancaster IV and V. Later, the Avro Shackleton kept the lineage going for further decades until as late as 1992. There was also a transport aircraft development, with four war surplus Lancasters being converted at Bracebridge Heath, Lincolnshire, as freighters for a brief period of use by British South African Airways. More relevant was the utility transport Avro York, and also a civilian airliner derivative, the less successful Lancastrian. 'Tiger Force', had it matured, would have adopted in-flight refuelling, and post war four Lancaster-IIIs were experimentally converted by Flight Refuelling Limited, two as tankers and two as receiving aircraft. The tankers saw service during the Berlin airlift with 757 missions. Many more retired Lancasters were sold abroad, including Argentina and Egypt. The very last RAF Lancaster was utilised by Fighter Command in the photographic role before finally being put out to grass in 1954. It was the end of an era.

aircrew were awarded the British Empire's highest award for bravery in combat, these being (in alphabetical order): Squadron Leader Ian Willoughby Bazalgette; Wing Commander Guy Gibson; Warrant Officer Norman Cyril Jackson; Pilot Officer Andrew Mynarski; Squadron Leader John Dering Nettleton; Squadron Leader Robert Anthony Maurice Palmer; Flight Lieutenant William Reid and Flight Sergeant George Thompson.

Each Lancaster cost around £45,000 to £50,000. To put this in context a contemporary modern battleship of the *King George V* class cost about £8,000,000, so for each battleship 160 Lancasters could have been built. To put it another way, the 7,377 Lancasters cost the nation, £368,859,000, for which 46 brand new battleships could have been built instead of just the five that were actually constructed!

Visible under the belly of Lancaster R5727 is the FN64 ventral turret. It was rarely used and was often removed. This Lancaster initially served with 44 Squadron and eventually ended up in Canada as a pattern for Canadian production.

Lancaster, NF926, HA-X, of No. 218 Squadron displays the two yellow bars on her fins indicating a 'Gee-H' bombing leader. Part of No.3 Group, 'B' Flight converted from Stirlings to a mix of Lancaster B.I/IIIs at Woolfox Lodge in July 1944. It then moved to Methwold, followed by 'A' Flight in August. In December 1944 they then moved to Chedburgh and operated through to the end of the war. NF926 went missing on a raid to Vohwinkel in Germany on 31 December 1944.

Lancasters of No. 83 Squadron lining up for take-off for the third 1,000-Bomber Raid against Bremen on 25 June 1942. The nearest aircraft is R5620, OL-H, which had completed six operations and failed to return that night with its crew reported as killed in action. Note the crewman who has partly climbed through an upper fuselage hatch, giving a 'V' for Victory symbol for the photographer.

Crews of No. 106 Squadron walk away from Lancaster R5573, ZN-B. A close inspection reveals a non-standard bulged bomb bay, which was fitted to allow larger bombs to be tested in action. Originally a Manchester squadron at Coningsby, No.106 received its Lancasters in May 1942 and in October moved to Syerston where it stayed until late 1943, when a final move was made to Metheringham. R5573 was lost on operations on 9 July 1943.

A Lancaster is silhouetted over the burning city of Hannover in October 1943.

This No. 44 (Rhodesia) Squadron Lancaster, KM-J, was badly damaged by a German night fighter over Peenemünde on 19 August 1943.

Lancaster DV305, BQ-O, of No. 550 Squadron, was attacked from the rear by a German night fighter over Berlin on 31 January 1944 and both its gunners were killed.

Left: Lancaster AA-A of No. 75 (New Zealand) Squadron pictured flying over the oil storage depot at Bec D'Ambes on 4 August 1944. Part of No.3 and 5 Groups, the squadron formed at Mepal in March 1944 having replaced its Stirlings from its No.3 Group squadron. In late March it was operating a mix of Lancaster B.1/IIIs and commenced its first operations. It then moved to Spilsby in 1945 which resulted in a transfer to Tiger Force as part of No.5 Group. Tiger Force, also known as the VLR Bomber Force, was the name given to a World War II British Commonwealth long-range heavy bomber force, formed in 1945, from squadrons serving with RAF Bomber Command in Europe, for proposed use against targets in Japan. The unit was scheduled to be redeployed to the Pacific theatre in the lead-up to the Allies' proposed invasion of Japan. The Force was disbanded after the bombing of Hiroshima and Nagasaki ended the war.

Right: With bomb doors open, a Lancaster flies over a bomb-blasted Calais on 25 September 1944. By this stage of the war, it was sufficiently safe for RAF night bombers to operate in daylight operations.

A No.103 Squadron Lancaster
photographed during a raid over the
V-weapons site at Wizernes, 20 July 1944.
Part of No.1 Group, the squadron replaced
its Halifaxes with Lancasters in November
1942 at Elsham Wolds. No.103 changed
its nameplate in November 1945 to
become No.57 Squadron.

The specially constructed U-boat
pens had extremely thick
concrete roofs, which could only
be penetrated by the 'Tallboy' and
'Grand-Slam' bombs introduced
later in the war. This hole at
Farge was made by a 22,000 lb
'Grand Slam'.

A Lancaster crew pose with a trophy of its raid on the pocket battleship, Admiral Scheer in Kiel harbour on 9 April 1945.

Two of No. 106 Squadron's armourers prepare to hoist a 1,000 lb bomb into the bomb bay of a Lancaster.

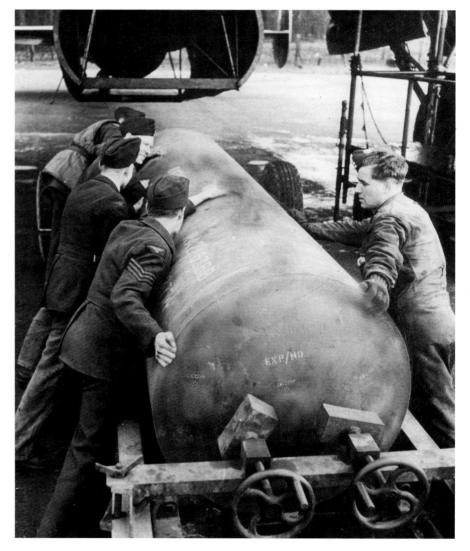

Ground crew haul an 8,000 lb 'Cookie' towards a Lancaster's open bomb bay.

Airmen of No. 460 Squadron sit on 500 lb bombs in front of Lancaster AR-Q, Q for Queenie. This RAAF squadron was part of No.1 Group and replaced its Halifaxes with Lancaster B.Is in October 1942. It eventually used a mix of B.I or IIIs. It moved to Binbrook in May 1943 where the code was changed from UV to AR, and then moved to East Kirkby in July 1945. The last flight carried out by the squadron was in October that year when RF191 photographed the Australian War Memorial in France.

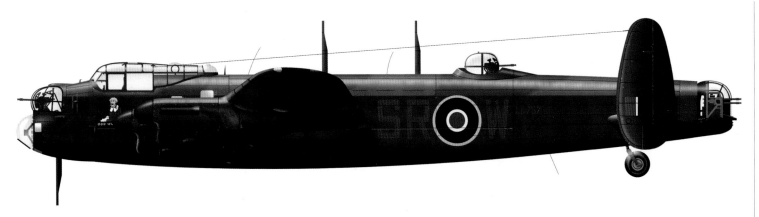

'Oor Wullie', an ABC (Airborne Cigar) Avro Lancaster B.I, LL757,SR-W, of No.101 Squadron. 1944.

Below: Lancaster B.I, LL757, SR-W, of No.101 Squadron, is fitted with Airborne Cigar (ABC) equipment to jam the Luftwaffe night fighters' radio control channels. Note the two large aerials extending above the fuselage, a distinctive feature of this device. An additional eighth crew member was added who was able to speak German and during an operation, was able to jam German ground-to-air radio transmissions and disrupt the German communication.

101 Squadron was the only squadron to utilise such equipment: as such they flew more operations, but also suffered heavier losses, than most other squadrons of No.1 Group. No.101 Squadron acquired its Lancasters in October 1942 at Elsham Wolds. In 1943 it moved to Ludford Magna and on to Binbrook in October 1945. It operated a mix of Lancaster B.I, III, VII and Xs. LL757 joined the unit in April 1944 and was lost on operations on 30 August 1944.

Three photographs of an ABC-equipped Lancaster B.I, NG128, SR-B of No.101 Squadron. Two of these images show it dropping incendiary bombs during a daylight raid over Duisburg on 14 October 1944. The photograph (top) shows an initial shower of 4 lb incendiaries being dropped which was then followed by a swarm of 14 lb incendiaries accompanied by a 4,000 lb H.C. bomb (above right). NG128 survived the war and was scrapped in January 1947.

Left: A 500 lb bomb on a bomb trolley appears to be at the centre of a light moment between a senior Army officer and a Group Captain, prior to them being loaded into a Lancaster.

Right: The United States on several occasions supplied bombs to RAF Bomber Command when its supplies ran short. Here RAF armourers are fitting American 'square tails' to bombs, which were not ideally suited for fitting into the RAF bombers' bomb bays.

890 LSGN 19-7-44 //8" 15000'← 090° 1559 MONT CANDON
Z 11x1000 : 3x500 : TYPE 14-2 secs : S/L SOOBY : Z 582

Seen here are 11 x 1000 lb and 3 x 500 lb
bombs being dropped from a No. 582
Squadron Lancaster over Mont Candon
on 19 July 1944. Note the both round
and US square tailed bombs.

An armourer helps to hoist a very
muddy incendiary container into
the bomb bay of a Lancaster.

A 12,000 lb HC bomb pictured
in front of a No. 617 Squadron
Lancaster before the ill-fated
Dortmund-Ems raid.

Squadron Leader John Cockshott of 617 Squadron flies over the Arbergen railway bridge in Lancaster B.1 Special, PD114, as the first bombs start to explode on the target on 21 March 1945. This aircraft survived the war and was scrapped in May 1947.

Lancasters of No. 622 Squadron taxi towards their take-off position for a daylight raid on Essen on 25 October 1944. Part of No.3 Group, the squadron formed at Mildenhall in June 1944 operating B.IIIs. It disbanded in August 1945.

Graceful but lethal – a Lancaster is silhouetted above the cloud as it drops its bombload on a V-1 site in France in late July 1944. In that year, the usually nocturnal Lancasters began operating in daylight due to growing Allied air superiority.

The city of Dresden burns during the heavy raid of 13 February 1945.

PA329 QR-K of 60 Squadron wears the high visibility white codes and underwing serials introduced just after the war to discourage low-level flying! Such markings are indicative of a post-war photograph. By war's end, 60 Squadron held the distinction of having flown more raids with the Lancaster than any other squadron in Bomber Command.

One of the most famous surviving Lancasters is R5868, PO-S of 467 Squadron RAAF. The nose carries the famous Hermann Göring boast to the German people "No enemy plane shall fly over the Reich Territory" - it also carries the impressive tally of over 100 mission symbols - the latter rising to 137. This Lancaster B.I originally served with 83 Squadron as OL-Q, and is now preserved at the RAF Museum in Hendon in North London. The photograph shows air and ground crew celebrating the completion of her 100th mission on 12 May 1944.

A beautiful air-to-air view of LM418, PG-S of 619 Squadron while on a training flight – note the lack of guns on the dorsal turret and the general toll operations took on the finish of the aircraft.

A WAAF driver tows DV238 of 49 Squadron to its hard standing. Based at Scampton, the Lancasters of this squadron later moved to Dunholme Lodge, Fiskerton and Fulbeck by October 1944. Its last wartime base was Syderston in April 1945 with moves to Mepal in January 1946 and Upwood several months later.

Heavy snow rarely held up
Bomber Command operations
for very long. With no shortage
of manpower, a bomber airfield
could have its runways cleared
within a few hours.

Serenely majestic in her element in an unthreatening sky. Yet Lancaster, LM446, PG-H, of 619 Squadron was lost on 9/10 May 1944 over Gennevilliers during a raid to bomb an engine factory – one of five Lancasters lost that night.

Air and ground crew of 460 Squadron RAAF, pose for the press with Q-Queenie at Binbrook in 1944. The large circle on the nose is a gas detection patch, common on many 1 Group Lancasters. The lack of these patches on any other Group's aircraft suggests that 1 Group would have been tasked with carrying chemical weapons should the need have arisen.

Right: An uncommon sight of Lancasters in a loose line astern formation – probably practising for a flypast.

Right: Veteran Lancaster L7580, EM-O, of 207 Squadron on display to thousands in Trafalgar Square on 7 March 1943 during a "Wings for Victory Week" for which the target was £150,000,000 in War savings. The amount raised so far at the time the photograph was taken, £30,111,150, can be seen on the side of the building, below left of the Lancaster. L7580 was an early production Lancaster and had an uneventful war, serving most of her time with 207 Squadron - though she had a code change later to become EM-C. The aircraft was SOC (struck off charge) in November 1945.

'Operation Manna' saw hundreds of Lancasters involved with dropping food supplies to the starving people of Holland in early May 1945. This aircraft is believed to be JB613 of 150 Squadron. This Lancaster had a chequered operational career - serving with 460 Squadron, 38 MU (Maintenance Unit), 625 Squadron and 150 squadron before being SOC (struck off charge) in December 1945.

Lancasters were also involved in 'Operation Dodge', the repatriation of thousands of Allied troops from Italy at the end of the war.

'A less deadly cargo' - ground crew load food supplies into the belly of a Lancaster destined for Holland as part of 'Operation Manna'. Between 29 April and 8 May 1945, Lancaster bombers dropped food into parts of the occupied Netherlands, with the acquiescence of the occupying German forces, to feed people who were in danger of starvation in the Dutch famine. The operation was named after the food which miraculously appeared for the Israelites in the book of Exodus, called Manna. During the operation, Bomber Command delivered 6,680 tons of food. The bombers were used to dropping bombs from 19,500 ft. but this time they had to do their dropping from a height of 500 ft, some even as low as 395 ft. The idea was for people to gather and redistribute the food, but some could not resist eating straight away, which caused some people to become sick and vomit, a result that fatty food can have in starved bodies. On the other hand, the just distribution took as long as ten days, as a result of which some got the food only after the liberation. Nevertheless, many lives were saved and another effect was that it gave hope and the feeling that the war would soon be over.

Late war and post-war development

A post-war formation of No. 35 Squadron Lancasters carrying the unit code TL, in their black and white 'Tiger Force' camouflage schemes. The squadron was chosen to undertake the RAF's first post-war goodwill tour of the United States.

Bottom left: A Lancaster B.VII, NX727, of No. 38 Squadron with the repositioned Martin mid-upper turret.

Below: This Lancaster B.IV, PW925, was essentially the prototype for the Lincoln.

This photograph of a Lincoln B.II, RF570, shows the extended wingtips and redesigned forward nose which were the main visual differences between the Lincoln and the Lancaster. This Lincoln is equiped with H2S Mk.IV A, officially known as B.2/4A. At this time, Bomber Command had dropped using unit code letters in place of using the aircraft serial number in a large format on the rear fuselage.

The Avro Shackleton was designed by Roy Chadwick under the designation Avro Type 696. It was based on the Avro Lincoln which, itself was a derivative of the Avro Lancaster bomber. The design was initially referred to, during development, as the Lincoln ASR.3 and took the Avro Lincoln's wings and landing gear, mating them with a new fuselage. The power was provided by four Rolls-Royce Griffon engines fitted with 13 ft. contra-rotating propellers which created a distinctive high-tone engine noise, adding possible deafness to the hazards of the crews. The first test flight took place during March 1949 with the first front-line aircraft being delivered to Coastal Command in April 1951. The aircraft made its operational debut during the Suez Crisis which began on 29 October 1956. In the ASW (Anti Submarine Warfare) role, the Shackleton M.R.1 carried both types of sonobuoy (acoustic anti-submarine detection), ESM (Electronic Warfare Support Measures), an Autolycus (diesel fume detection system) and, for a short time, an unreliable magnetic anomaly detector (MAD) system. Ordnance could be either nine bombs, or three torpedoes or depth charges, plus 20 mm cannon defensive armament.

The M.R.2 was an improved version which evolved from feedback via the crews on operations and was considered by many to be the definitive variant. The radome (radar dome) was moved from the nose to a ventral position, which improved all-round coverage and also reduced the risk of bird-strikes. Both the nose and tail sections were lengthened and the tail planes were also redesigned and the weak undercarriage strengthened.

The M.R.3 was a further redesign, mainly in response to crew complaints. A new tricycle undercarriage was installed and the fuselage was increased in all main dimensions, plus new wings with better ailerons and fuel tip tanks were also added. As a sop to the crews, often on fifteen-hour flights, the sound deadening was improved and a proper galley and sleeping space were also provided. The total take-off weight had risen by over 30,000 lb and assistance from Armstrong Siddeley Viper Mk.203 turbojets needed for take-off (JATO) was provided. All this put extra strain on the airframe, reducing the life-span of the Mk. III Shackletons so much that they were outlived by the earlier Mk. IIs.

All marks were powered by Rolls-Royce Griffon engines, which were thirsty for fuel and oil, very noisy and temperamental plus had high-maintenance needs. In 1961, MR.2's engines needed major

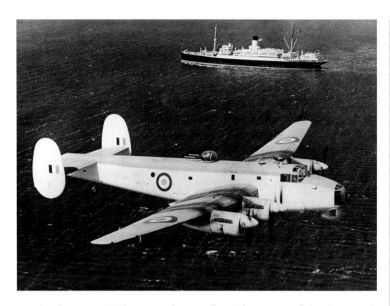

Shackleton M.R.1

overhauls every 400 hours and went through a spate of ejecting spark plugs from their cylinder heads. It was not unusual to see one engine changed every day in a unit of six aircraft. They were constantly on the cusp of being replaced, but even the potentially improved Napier Nomad engine never quite happened.

A replacement for the Shackleton was first discussed in the early 1960s and the arrival of the Hawker-Siddeley Nimrod in 1969 should have seen the end for the Shackleton in most roles. However it continued as the main SAR (Submarine Aerial Reconnaissance) aircraft until 1972. The intention to finally retire the aircraft was then thwarted by the need for AEW (Airborne Early Warning) coverage in the North Sea and northern Atlantic following the retirement of the Fairey Gannet. The disastrous Nimrod AEW replacement programme dragged on and on and the eventual successor to the Shackleton did not arrive until the RAF finally abandoned the Nimrod AEW and purchased the Boeing E-3 Sentry, a modified Boeing 707-310B fitted with AWACS (Airborne Warning And Control System), in 1991.

A total of 185 Shackletons were built between 1951 and 1958 with around twelve still believed to be intact, mainly on display in various museums, with one still flying. Although the joke has been applied to several aircraft, the Shackleton was often described as "a hundred thousand rivets flying in loose formation".

Right: The Shackleton M.R.2 WR966 circa 1962, shows the principal differences between it and the M.R.1 repositioned radome under the rear fuselage, lengthened nose and tail sections incorporating new clear vision sections and a twin retractable tail-wheel.

Below right: The Avro 691 Lancastrian was a passenger and mail transport aircraft developed from the Avro Lancaster bomber. the Lancastrian was very similar to the Lancaster, differing primarily in having all of the armament removed and faired over, and the replacement of the glazed nose with a streamlined "solid" model. In 1945, deliveries commenced of 30 British-built Lancastrians for BOAC. On a demonstration flight on 23 April 1945, G-AGLF flew 13,500 miles (21,700 km) from England to Auckland, New Zealand in three days, 14 hours at an average speed of 220 mph (354 km/h).

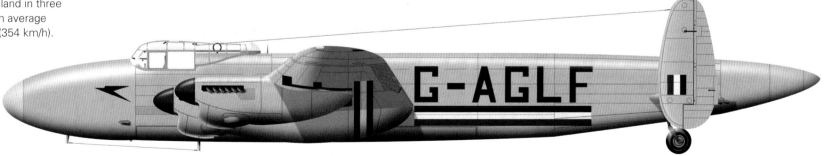

This Avro Lancastrian, G-AGLF, was with BOAC during 1945.

The Lancaster acquired legendary status among heavy bomber aficionados as a result of the Ministry of Information's widespread distribution of film and leaflets during the war. The appearance of numerous popular war memoirs and accounts, such as Guy Gibson's Enemy Coast Ahead *and Paul Brickhill's* The Dam Busters, *was reinforced post war by iconic films which took up the wartime themes of stoic and self-deprecating 'Bomber Boys" courage typified by Emeric Pressburger's* One of Our Aircraft is Missing. *In more recent years the inclusion of one Lancaster bomber in the Battle of Britain Memorial Flight, however incongruous, has merely reinforced her unique status and affection in the general public's overall psyche, most of whom have little or no idea of the differing roles performed by a Spitfire and Hurricane on one hand and a Lancaster on the other, save that they 'won the war'. Some twenty-four Lancasters, a fraction of the thousands built, have been preserved restored or exist in one form or another, and while only a pair remain in flying condition, and only a trio actually saw combat, it is enough to demonstrate even to cynical modern eyes what a remarkable flying machine the Lancaster was.*

Left: The forward cockpit of Lancaster NX611, a Mk.VII (FE) at East Kirkby in Lincolnshire.

AS with all historical aircraft of the Second World War period, those examples that have been preserved are not always those with the greatest historical battle records. It is inevitable that those completed late and either used on post-war duties and therefore kept in good condition, or placed in reserve and kept pristine, would survive, while war-weary aircraft would quickly find their way to the scrapyards. Nonetheless, the Lancaster is fortunate in that machines of various Marks have managed to be salvaged or rebuilt to give a very good mix across the range.

Only two of the Lancasters of the twenty-odd examples still available for viewing are in flyable condition, and, naturally these arouse the most interest in the public at large. Historical buffs and aviation experts are more likely to be drawn to these few veterans of combat, whose war records enshrine the sacrifice and ethos of Bomber Command, and, thankfully, there are a few of these also which can be accessed. Finally, with the great resurgence of interest in the last two decades, coupled with the money to finance it, many wrecks, abandoned and almost forgotten for decades, are now located and identified and await transportation and careful reassembly in order to join the ranks of the static exhibits. The Royal Canadian Air Force, and its combined Armed Force successor, was one of the operators that kept the Lancaster in the air for longer than most, where it served with their Maritime Air Command unit at Downsview until as late as 1964. Not surprisingly then, by far the greatest concentration of saved and salvageable Lancasters are to be found there. Interest has also been aroused in wrecks and possible survivals from the *Tirpitz* raids in both Scandinavia and in North Russia and these areas might yet yield new finds in the years ahead.

Right: Lancaster B. I, PA474, has been part of the Battle of Britain Memorial Flight since 1973. The camouflage scheme is periodically changed to represent notable Lancasters. This view shows her when she was painted to represent KM-B, the Lancaster flown by Sqn. Ldr. John Nettleton VC on the disastrous Augsburg raid in April 1942.

Here are the histories of just a few of the 'Preserved' Lancasters.

PA474:

Probably the most well known Lancaster in the United Kingdom is PA474, a B1 aircraft currently gracing the Battle of Britain Memorial Flight and based, appropriately enough, at Coningsby in Lincolnshire. A product of the late war programme, PA474 came off the assembly line at the Chester works of Vickers Armstrong when the European air war was already a memory. She was earmarked to join one of the squadrons forming to participate in the final drive on, and planned invasion of Japan, with Tiger Force, but, with a mere three hours flying time under her belt, the surrender in Tokyo Bay put paid to the invasion and she was put into reserve. No. 38 Maintenance Unit (MU) at Llandow briefly became her new abode, but she was rescued from this ignominy since, being in prime condition, she was selected for refurbishment for a very different career.

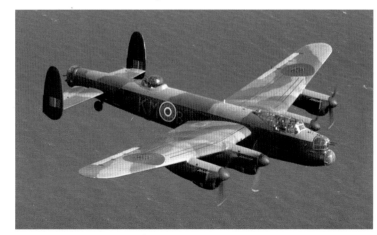

Delivered into No. 82 Squadron RAF, she was flown to the West African town Takordai, a well known wartime air staging post, which was being used by a detachment to carry out aerial photographic surveying work in that region.

On completion of this task, PA474 was destined to be converted a second time, this time into a drone aircraft by Flight Refuelling Limited, based at Tarrant Rushton in England. Before work commenced, however, another change of plan saw her moved over to Cranfield airfield near Bedford, where she became part of the establishment of the College of Aeronautics as a flying test-bed. During this period of her employment she was utilised to take aloft various experimental wing forms then under development for more

contemporary aircraft, to see how they performed. This vital duty kept her gainfully employed while most of her sister Lancasters had long faded away. To keep her flying, essential parts and fittings had to be stocked and this was to prove invaluable when her final future came to be decided, when she once more reverted to RAF control in 1964.

Again PA474 failed to follow the score written for her, which was to become a static display exhibit at the new RAF Museum being planned for the old Hendon airfield site in north-west London. In the interim, the Lancaster veteran was put under the care and maintenance of the Air Historical Branch. She was painted up in 'proper' Bomber Command war configuration and stored at

Lancaster B. I, PA474, is at the time of writing (but not above) wearing the colours of EE139 'Phantom of the Ruhr' (see the Foreword), bearing the codes HW-R on the port side and BQ-B on the starboard side.

Wroughton. Here she was safe from wind and weather, but soon afterwards a change of policy saw her move back to Bedfordshire, this time to RAF Henlow, where she was parked outside and fully exposed to the Home Counties elements. Not surprisingly, she began to suffer and there were fears that she would deteriorate beyond saving. Fortunately, some people with a little more awareness and care for history than the AHB mandarins, including the Commanding Officer of No. 44 Squadron, offered to take better care of such a unique aircraft and she was flown up to Waddington on 18 August 1965, where she was promised hangar accommodation once more.

At Waddington a full inspection revealed the old matron to be still in control of most of her faculties and she was deemed not only salvable, but, with a little loving care and attention, capable of being returned to full airworthiness. No. 44 Squadron was as good as its word and to many people's amazement and delight, PA474 was permitted by the hitherto largely indifferent 'powers-that-be' to make commemorative flights when conditions allowed. She soon became a welcome addition to any major Air Show and was much in demand, embarrassingly so for the Squadron, who had other duties to attend to.

It was decided in the early 1970s that the specialist care and attention the stately old Lancaster required were to be found with the teams which nurtured the Supermarine Spitfire and Hawker Hurricane fighter aircraft of the Battle of Britain Memorial Flight, based at RAF Coltishall, just north of Norwich in Norfolk, and she joined that distinguished band in November 1973. Less than three years later, in March 1976, the whole flight was transferred north to Coningsby and for the thirty-plus years since, she has hardly ever been grounded. A further refurbishment to keep her flying was undertaken at RAF St. Athan between 1995 and 1996 and, more than a decade on, even with the undercarriage of a Lincoln derivative and the main-wheels of a Shackleton derivative, plus a varied assortment of engines, she is still stunning generations who have no memory or concept of propeller-driven aircraft or her original conceived role, with her sheer presence, sound and power. Lancaster PA474, as the *City of Lincoln* and coded KM-B, has become more than a flying veteran, she has become a veritable Institution.

FM213:

The second of only two Lancasters still flying today, this B.X Mark machine belongs to the Canadian Warplane Heritage Museum,

located at Hamilton, Ontario. This aircraft is FM213, a Mk. X machine, which originally served with the RCAF's No. 107 Rescue Unit. She was retired in 1964 and was taken over as a static display by the Royal Canadian Legion's Goderick Branch. This ensured her further survival but she deteriorated down the years before being saved in 1977 by her present owners. Although most people considered she would never again be airworthy, years of dedicated care restored her to full flying status and, on 23 September 1988, she was again declared fully operational.

She carries the civilian registration C-GVRA for flying purposes, but is painted up as Lancaster VR-A, KB726 to commemorate the famous wartime hero who was posthumously awarded the Victoria Cross, twenty-seven year old Andrew Charles Mynarski, son of a Polish immigrant settled in Winnipeg, Manitoba. He had served briefly in the Royal Winnipeg Rifles before joining the RCAF at the age of twenty-four. After training he was posted to No. 9 Squadron in October 1943, before transferring to No. 419 (Moose) Squadron, RCAF.

On the night of 12/13 June No. 419 Squadron, took part in an attack on the strategically important rail yard at Cambrai, France, through which war supplies and reinforcements were being fed to the German troops opposing the breakout from the Normandy beachhead by the Allied armies. Mynarski was a wireless operator/air gunner who had only joined the squadron at Middleton St. George in March. On this night, the crew's thirteenth mission, he was flying as the mid-upper gunner in a new Lancaster, piloted by Art de Bryne, but was unable to engage a German Junkers Ju 88 night fighter, which attacked from below and astern, the Lancaster's 'blind spot'. Raked by cannon shells, both the port engines were put out of action and the wing was set ablaze. The damage to the engines caused the hydraulic power to the rear turret to also fail and it could not rotate, trapping its occupant. Below and to the immediate rear of Mynarski's position, shells also set ablaze the aircraft's rear fuselage and quickly took hold. The aircraft was clearly doomed and the aircrew were ordered to bail out.

On his way to the escape hatch, Mynarski noticed the dire situation of his rear gunner, Pat Brophy, who, in his frantic efforts to manually exit the locked-up turret had broken the gear totally and was firmly trapped. Despite the fact that the fuselage was ablaze between him and the rear turret, Mynarski forced his way through,

This beautifully preserved
Lancaster is NX611, a Mk.VII (FE)
which at the time of writing
currently resides at East Kirkby
in Lincolnshire.

NX611 wears the DX codes of
No. 57 Squadron on her starboard
side and the LE codes of No. 630
Squadron on the port.

NX611 is frequently run up
for the benefit of the public,
an impressive sight and sound
at any time!

Left: The Flight Engineer's view of the instrument panel of NX611, with the entrance to the bomb aimer's position at bottom right.

A detailed view of the flap interior of NX611. Note how the engine rear nacelle folded into itself when the flaps were lowered.

NX611 is fitted with an FN 82 rear turret housing 2 x 0.5 inch Browning machine guns.

The bombing camera aperture in the nose of NX611. It was in this hole that the Dambuster Lancasters carried their forward spotlight.

A view aft of NX611's capacious, but empty, bomb-bay.

setting ablaze his uniform and own parachute in the process. He made determined attempts to free the mechanism, but in vain. Realising that he himself was probably doomed, the rear gunner indicated to Mynarski that he should abandon further attempts, as the bomber was now on the way down, and save himself if he still could. Mynarski managed to reach the hatch and gave the rear gunner a final salute at attention before leaving the blazing aircraft. Alas, with his parachute ablaze and clothes burning fiercely, he made a fiery descent, which was observed by several French civilians who ran to his aid. They found him, but he was so severely burnt all over his upper body that he died within a few hours, before he could receive full medical help.

His courage would have gone unnoticed, just another Lancaster victim among many thousands of such young men, but for the rear gunner himself. As the Lancaster ploughed blazing into the ground, but in a shallow approach, two of the bombs still on board detonated on impact. Some quirk of fate saved Brophy from his seemingly irretrievable death situation for the explosions tossed him clear of the turret and he was rescued alive. His stopped wristwatch showed 0213 hrs on Friday 13 June. He subsequently testified to the gallant efforts of Mynarski who could have saved himself but chose to try and save a comrade. The award of the VC was rarely more warranted and he was also posthumously promoted to Pilot Officer.

Since 1988 FM213 has had a fairly regular and full flying programme, always by highly experienced pilots, including more than 600 hours by Cy Dunbar, who had first flown Lancasters in January 1955 with No. 2 Maritime Operational Training Unit at Summerside, Prince Edward Island, Canada. However, the years have again taken their toll and the summer of 1996 marked the final time the 'Mynarski Lancaster' took part in a full circuit tour. She still flies occasionally, locally around the Hamilton area and long may she continue to do so.

R5868:

Among the static display Lancasters, R5868 is the most-visited and also, as an Metropolitan Vickers-built Mk.1 aircraft from an original Avro Manchester airframe, and with a proud service and combat record of 137 operations, among the most worthy survivors on show. Her prime location, at the famed Royal Air Force Museum at Hendon, London, ensures she is probably among the most-visited of

such machines. Delivered as early as June 1942 and initially flying as *Q-Queenie,* she served with No. 83 Squadron RAF based at RAF Scampton. She made her debut on the night of 8/9 July 1942, with an attack against the main German naval base of Wilhelmshaven. After many more missions with the squadron, later based at RAF Wyton, near Huntingdon, where she operated with the newly-formed Pathfinder Force, she was subsequently transferred, in August 1943, to No. 463 RAAF Squadron based at Bottesford, as their *S-Sugar* (PO-S) and was the first Lancaster to survive one hundred operations – a rarity indeed. The fact that she did so after flak damage over Berlin and a mid-air collision with another Lancaster followed by a crash-landing and a virtual rebuilding, speaks volumes for the ruggedness of the Lancaster. She resumed operations in February 1945, ending her fighting career with No. 467 RAAF Squadron based at RAF Waddington, with her final combat mission flown on 23 April 1945.

R5868 is therefore the oldest of all the veteran Lancasters and had some 500 operational hours on the clock when most contemporaries were barely surviving a single tour. Despite this fact, the post-war years saw her stored at Wroughton for a decade before someone realised her rarity value and, in 1956, assigned her to the RAF Historical Aircraft Collection. Even then she was used merely as a gate guard at RAF Scampton, Lincolnshire, for some years and it was not until the re-allocation of the earmarked PA474 elsewhere, that R5868 was substituted as the RAF Museum's Lancaster, finally a sensible choice. She underwent significant restoration at Hendon and emerged fully refurbished and gleaming to take her due place at the inauguration of the Museum in November 1972.

NX622:

This B.VII aircraft was built by Austin Motors at Longbridge and completed to the FE specification in May 1945 and taken on charge by No. 38 Maintenance Unit (MU) at RAF Llandow, Wales. With the unexpected termination of the Pacific War in July, all these aircraft were surplus to requirements and as many of the special Far Eastern specifications were deemed unnecessary, she was sent back to the plant to have them stripped out before being returned to No. 38 MU for storage, after a flying life of just seven hours.

She remained unwanted in her Welsh retreat until 1951 when, as part of the early Cold War scare, she was one of 54 preserved Lancasters bulk purchased for Western Union use as a Maritime

Reconnaissance aircraft for the French Navy's land-based air arm, *L'Aeronautique Navale*. The threat of the Soviet Union's five hundred-plus submarines was considered a real one at the time, for the Royal Navy had been enormously reduced and anti-submarine warships had largely been scrapped post-war. Great Britain's allies in Europe, after six years of occupation, also had little left to combat such a large potentially lethal force and the United States was still standing aloof, this being the pre-NATO era. Pending more modern aircraft, and adaptations like the Shackleton, the French purchase of the Lancasters was a necessary stopgap measure.

NX622 was therefore transported over to Avro's plant for the makeover from heavy bomber to anti-submarine patrol aircraft; the dorsal turret was removed, and ASV radar installed along with other over-water equipment and the fitting of auxiliary fuel tanks. She was also given a new deep-water blue paint scheme to replace the RAF drab. Thus converted, the aircraft received a brand new serial number, WU16 (Western Union No. 16) and was handed over to the French Navy on 18 June 1952. Her new owners flew her to Lann Bihouee airfield, close to the great naval base of L'Orient in Brittany, where she joined *Flotille* 24F and commenced extensive patrolling. Further updating was done at Cuers NAS, Toulon, and airborne radar was fitted, after which she resumed her duties but with *Flotille* 25F. After some 1,300 hours had been logged a more extensive refit was carried out at Le Bourget, Paris by UTA mechanics.

Upon upgrading, the French Navy transferred WU16 to the Pacific, so she eventually reached her original destination, joining Air Support Squadron 9S based at Tontouta in New Caledonia in May 1957. In 1959 a further routine 600-hour airframe and 200-hour engine overhaul took place, this time by the Fairey Aviation Company at Bankstown, New South Wales and then she carried on in the same role until 1961, when all four Merlins, after ten years' hard work, were replaced. The end of their useful employment was now imminent for spare parts were now at a premium. The scrap heap beckoned but salvation came in the form of the Royal Australian Air Force Association in Perth, many of whose members had fond memories of the Lancaster during the Second World War.

The Association approached the French Ambassador and after some five days of negotiations, it was agreed that the *Aéronavale's* five-man crew would fly the aircraft to Sydney and then up to Kingston Smith Airport, Perth via Adelaide. This programme duly followed

and WU16 arrived at Perth on Saturday 1 December 1962. This unique acquisition cost the Association just £620! The Lancaster was put on display at the airport, but was vandalised internally by locals. Eventually No/26 City of Perth Squadron, Citizen's Air Force volunteers repainted her white livery with Bomber Command colours and she re-assumed her old serial NX622, along with the totally bogus code letters AF-C. Here she stayed, with a steel structure supporting her undercarriage, for seventeen years exposed to the elements and naturally, deteriorated.

The planned airport expansion mooted in 1978 led to a demand by the Department of Civil Aviation for the Lancaster to be either moved or scrapped and she was advertised for sale. However, funds were forthcoming from the State and she was partially dismantled and towed away to join a dozen other veterans at Bull Creek, arriving on 19 August 1979. She again stood in the open on a concrete pad by the hangar entrance until 1984, when completion of a larger hangar enabled her to be finally moved inside.

With the skilled input of the Midland Technical School under pilot Derek McPhail extensive and detailed restoration work took place and she was painted once more under the auspices of Al Clarke, to represent *D-for-Dog* (JO-D) a wartime Lancaster that had flown 93 combat sorties, mainly with West Australian aircrew.

Summary of Preservations
Flying Survivors:

PA474	B1	RAF Battle of Britain Memorial Flight, Coningsby, Lincs, UK
FM213	BX	Canadian Warplane Heritage Museum, Hamilton, Ont, Canada

Non-Flying Preservations:

R5868	B.1	RAF Museum, Hendon, London
W4783	B.1	Australian War Museum, Canberra, A.C.T., Australia
W4964	B.1	Newark Air Museum, Notts, UK
DV372	B.1	Imperial War Museum, London
NX611	B.VII	Lincolnshire Aviation Heritage Centre, East Kirkby, Lincs, UK

NX622	B.VII	Aviation Heritage Museum, Bull Creek, Perth, WA, Australia
NX664	B.VII	Ailes Anciennes, Paris, France
NX665	B.VII	Museum of Transport and Technology, Auckland, NZ
FM104	B.X	National Exhibition Ground, Toronto, Ont, Canada
FM136	B.X	Calgary Aerospace Museum, Calgary, Alberta, Canada
FM159	B.X	Lancaster Society Museum, Nanton, Alberta, Canada
FM212	B.X	City of Windsor Airport, Windsor, Ont, Canada
KB839	B.X	Canadian Forces Base, Greenwood, Newfoundland, Canada
KB848	B.X	St. Jacques Airport, Edmunston, New Brunswick, Canada
KB889	B.X	Imperial War Museum, Duxford, Cambs. UK
KB994	B.X	National Aviation Museum Rockliffe, Ottawa, Canada
KB976	B.X	Fantasy of Flight, Weeks Air Museum, Polk City, Florida, USA

Serial unknown	B.X	Menihek, NW Territory, Canada
Serial unknown	B.III	North Russia, ex-*Tirpitz* attack, various unconfirmed remains

Remains pending rebuilding:

NF920	B.1	Sweden KC-E Porjus, Jokkmokk, Sweden. *Easy Elsie*
FM118	B.X	Nanton, recovered ex-Shilo CFB Gunnery Range, Manitoba
FM221	B.X	Resolute Bay, Nunavut, NW Territory, Canada
KB882	B.X	ex-NA-R. St. Jacques Airport, New Brunswick, Canada
KB885	B.X	RCAF Red Deer, Alberta, Canada
KB944	B.X	Ex-NA-P National Aeronautical Collection, Rockcliffe, Canada
KB999	B.X	Ex-VR-M, *Malton Mike*, Churchill, Manitoba, Canada